THE CRUCIBLE

Arthur Miller

SPARK PUBLISHING

SPARKNOTES is a registered trademark of SparkNotes LLC

Spark Publishing
A Division of Barnes & Noble
120 Fifth Avenue
New York, NY 10011
www.sparknotes.com

ISBN-13: 978-1-4114-0365-9
ISBN-10: 1-4114-0365-7

Please submit changes or report errors to www.sparknotes.com/errors.

Printed in the United States.

10

CONTENTS

CONTEXT   1

PLOT OVERVIEW   5

CHARACTER LIST   7

ANALYSIS OF MAJOR CHARACTERS   11
   JOHN PROCTOR   11
   ABIGAIL WILLIAMS   12
   REVEREND HALE   13

THEMES, MOTIFS & SYMBOLS   15
   INTOLERANCE   15
   HYSTERIA   15
   REPUTATION   16
   EMPOWERMENT   17
   ACCUSATIONS, CONFESSIONS, AND LEGAL PROCEEDINGS   17
   THE WITCH TRIALS AND MCCARTHYISM   18

SUMMARY & ANALYSIS   19
   ACT I: OPENING SCENE TO THE ENTRANCE OF
      JOHN PROCTOR   19
   ACT I: THE ENTRANCE OF JOHN PROCTOR TO THE
      ENTRANCE OF REVEREND HALE   22
   ACT I: THE ENTRANCE OF REVEREND HALE TO THE
      CLOSING SCENE   26
   ACT II   29
   ACT III   32
   ACT IV–EPILOGUE   35

IMPORTANT QUOTATIONS EXPLAINED   39

KEY FACTS   45

STUDY QUESTIONS   47

HOW TO WRITE LITERARY ANALYSIS   51
   THE LITERARY ESSAY: A STEP-BY-STEP GUIDE   51
   SUGGESTED ESSAY TOPICS   63
   A+ STUDENT ESSAY   64
   GLOSSARY OF LITERARY TERMS   66
   A NOTE ON PLAGIARISM   68

REVIEW & RESOURCES   69
   QUIZ   69
   SUGGESTIONS FOR FURTHER READING   74

CONTEXT

ARLY IN THE YEAR 1692, in the small Massachusetts village of Salem, a collection of girls fell ill, falling victim to hallucinations and seizures. In extremely religious Puritan New England, frightening or surprising occurrences were often attributed to the devil or his cohorts. The unfathomable sickness spurred fears of witchcraft, and it was not long before the girls, and then many other residents of Salem, began to accuse other villagers of consorting with devils and casting spells. Old grudges and jealousies spilled out into the open, fueling the atmosphere of hysteria. The Massachusetts government and judicial system, heavily influenced by religion, rolled into action. Within a few weeks, dozens of people were in jail on charges of witchcraft. By the time the fever had run its course, in late August 1692, nineteen people (and two dogs) had been convicted and hanged for witchcraft.

More than two centuries later, Arthur Miller was born in New York City on October 17, 1915. His career as a playwright began while he was a student at the University of Michigan. Several of his early works won prizes, and during his senior year, the Federal Theatre Project in Detroit performed one of his works. He produced his first great success, *All My Sons,* in 1947. Two years later, in 1949, Miller wrote *Death of a Salesman,* which won the Pulitzer Prize and transformed Miller into a national sensation. Many critics described *Death of a Salesman* as the first great American tragedy, and Miller gained an associated eminence as a man who understood the deep essence of the United States.

Drawing on research on the witch trials he had conducted while an undergraduate, Miller composed *The Crucible* in the early 1950s. Miller wrote the play during the brief ascendancy of Senator Joseph McCarthy, a demagogue whose vitriolic anti-Communism proved the spark needed to propel the United States into a dramatic and fractious anti-Communist fervor during these first tense years of the Cold War with the Soviet Union. Led by McCarthy, special congressional committees conducted highly controversial investigations intended to root out Communist sympathizers in the United States. As with the alleged witches of Salem, suspected Communists were encouraged to confess and to identify other Red sympathizers as means of escaping punishment. The policy resulted in a whirl-wind of accusations. As people began to realize that they might be condemned as Communists regardless of their innocence, many "cooperated," attempting to save themselves through false confessions, creating the image that the United States was overrun with Communists and perpetuating the hysteria. The liberal entertainment industry, in which Miller worked, was one of the chief targets of these "witch hunts," as their opponents termed them. Some cooperated; others, like Miller, refused to give in to questioning. Those who were revealed, falsely or legitimately, as Communists, and those who refused to incriminate their friends, saw their careers suffer, as they were blacklisted from potential jobs for many years afterward.

At the time of its first performance, in January of 1953, critics and cast alike perceived *The Crucible* as a direct attack on McCarthyism (the policy of sniffing out Communists). Its comparatively short run, compared with those of Miller's other works, was blamed on anti-Communist fervor. When Julius and Ethel Rosenberg were accused of spying for the Soviets and executed, the cast and audience of Miller's play observed a moment of silence. Still, there are difficulties with interpreting *The Crucible* as a strict allegorical treatment of 1950s McCarthyism. For one thing, there were, as far as one can tell, no actual witches or devil-worshipers in Salem. However, there were certainly Communists in 1950s America, and many of those who were lionized as victims of McCarthyism at the time, such as the Rosenbergs and Alger Hiss (a former State Department official), were later found to have been in the pay of the Soviet Union. Miller's Communist friends, then, were often less innocent than the victims of the Salem witch trials, like the stalwart Rebecca Nurse or the tragic John Proctor.

If Miller took unknowing liberties with the facts of his own era, he also played fast and loose with the historical record. The general outline of events in *The Crucible* corresponds to what happened in Salem of 1692, but Miller's characters are often composites. Furthermore, his central plot device—the affair between Abigail Williams and John Proctor—has no grounding in fact (Proctor was over sixty at the time of the trials, while Abigail was only eleven). Thus, Miller's decision to set sexual jealousy at the root of the hysteria constitutes a dramatic contrivance.

In an odd way, then, *The Crucible* is best read outside its historical context—not as a perfect allegory for anti-Communism, or as a faithful account of the Salem trials, but as a powerful and timeless depiction of how intolerance and hysteria can intersect and tear a community apart. In John Proctor, Miller gives the reader a marvelous tragic hero for any time—a flawed figure who finds his moral center just as everything is falling to pieces around him.

PLOT OVERVIEW

I
N THE PURITAN NEW ENGLAND TOWN of Salem, Massachusetts, a group of girls goes dancing in the forest with a black
slave named Tituba. While dancing, they are caught by the local minister, Reverend Parris. One of the girls, Parris's daughter Betty, falls into a coma-like state. A crowd gathers in the
Parris home while rumors of witchcraft fill the town. Having sent
for Reverend Hale, an expert on witchcraft, Parris questions Abigail
Williams, the girls' ringleader, about the events that took place in
the forest. Abigail, who is Parris's niece and ward, admits to doing
nothing beyond "dancing."

While Parris tries to calm the crowd that has gathered in his
home, Abigail talks to some of the other girls, telling them not to
admit to anything. John Proctor, a local farmer, then enters and
talks to Abigail alone. Unbeknownst to anyone else in the town,
while working in Proctor's home the previous year she engaged in
an affair with him, which led to her being fired by his wife, Elizabeth. Abigail still desires Proctor, but he fends her off and tells her to
end her foolishness with the girls.

Betty wakes up and begins screaming. Much of the crowd rushes
upstairs and gathers in her bedroom, arguing over whether she is
bewitched. A separate argument between Proctor, Parris, the argumentative Giles Corey, and the wealthy Thomas Putnam soon en-
sues. This dispute centers on money and land deeds, and it suggests
that deep fault lines run through the Salem community. As the men
argue, Reverend Hale arrives and examines Betty, while Proctor de-
parts. Hale quizzes Abigail about the girls' activities in the forest,
grows suspicious of her behavior, and demands to speak to Tituba.
After Parris and Hale interrogate her for a brief time, Tituba confesses to communing with the devil, and she hysterically accuses
various townsfolk of consorting with the devil. Suddenly, Abigail
joins her, confessing to having seen the devil conspiring and cavort-
ing with other townspeople. Betty joins them in naming witches,
and the crowd is thrown into an uproar.

A week later, alone in their farmhouse outside of town, John and
Elizabeth Proctor discuss the ongoing trials and the escalating number of townsfolk who have been accused of being witches. Elizabeth
urges her husband to denounce Abigail as a fraud; he refuses, and

she becomes jealous, accusing him of still harboring feelings for her. Mary Warren, their servant and one of Abigail's circle, returns from Salem with news that Elizabeth has been accused of witchcraft but the court did not pursue the accusation. Mary is sent up to bed, and John and Elizabeth continue their argument, only to be interrupted by a visit from Reverend Hale. While they discuss matters, Giles Corey and Francis Nurse come to the Proctor home with news that their wives have been arrested. Officers of the court suddenly arrive and arrest Elizabeth. After they have taken her, Proctor browbeats Mary, insisting that she must go to Salem and expose Abigail and the other girls as frauds.

The next day, Proctor brings Mary to court and tells Judge Danforth that she will testify that the girls are lying. Danforth is suspicious of Proctor's motives and tells Proctor, truthfully, that Elizabeth is pregnant and will be spared for a time. Proctor persists in his charge, convincing Danforth to allow Mary to testify. Mary tells the court that the girls are lying. When the girls are brought in, they turn the tables by accusing Mary of bewitching them. Furious, Proctor confesses his affair with Abigail and accuses her of being motivated by jealousy of his wife. To test Proctor's claim, Danforth summons Elizabeth and asks her if Proctor has been unfaithful to her. Despite her natural honesty, she lies to protect Proctor's honor, and Danforth denounces Proctor as a liar. Meanwhile, Abigail and the girls again pretend that Mary is bewitching them, and Mary breaks down and accuses Proctor of being a witch. Proctor rages against her and against the court. He is arrested, and Hale quits the proceedings.

The summer passes and autumn arrives. The witch trials have caused unrest in neighboring towns, and Danforth grows nervous. Abigail has run away, taking all of Parris's money with her. Hale, who has lost faith in the court, begs the accused witches to confess falsely in order to save their lives, but they refuse. Danforth, how-ever, has an idea: he asks Elizabeth to talk John into confessing, and she agrees. Conflicted, but desiring to live, John agrees to confess, and the officers of the court rejoice. But he refuses to incriminate anyone else, and when the court insists that the confession must be made public, Proctor grows angry, tears it up, and retracts his admission of guilt. Despite Hale's desperate pleas, Proctor goes to the gallows with the others, and the witch trials reach their awful conclusion.

CHARACTER LIST

John Proctor A local farmer who lives just outside town; Elizabeth Proctor's husband. A stern, harsh-tongued man, John hates hypocrisy. Nevertheless, he has a hidden sin—his affair with Abigail Williams—that proves his downfall. When the hysteria begins, he hesitates to expose Abigail as a fraud because he worries that his secret will be revealed and his good name ruined.

Abigail Williams Reverend Parris's niece. Abigail was once the servant for the Proctor household, but Elizabeth Proctor fired her after she discovered that Abigail was having an affair with her husband, John Proctor. Abigail is smart, wily, a good liar, and vindictive when crossed.

Reverend John Hale A young minister reputed to be an expert on witchcraft. Reverend Hale is called in to Salem to examine Parris's daughter Betty. Hale is a committed Christian and hater of witchcraft. His critical mind and intelligence save him from falling into blind fervor. His arrival sets the hysteria in motion, although he later regrets his actions and attempts to save the lives of those accused.

Elizabeth Proctor John Proctor's wife. Elizabeth fired Abigail when she discovered that her husband was having an affair with Abigail. Elizabeth is supremely virtuous, but often cold.

Reverend Parris The minister of Salem's church. Reverend Parris is a paranoid, power-hungry, yet oddly self-pitying figure. Many of the townsfolk, especially John Proctor, dislike him, and Parris is very concerned with building his position in the community.

Rebecca Nurse Francis Nurse's wife. Rebecca is a wise, sensible, and upright woman, held in tremendous regard by most of the Salem community. However, she falls victim to the hysteria when the Putnams accuse her of witchcraft and she refuses to confess.

Francis Nurse A wealthy, influential man in Salem. Nurse is well respected by most people in Salem, but is an enemy of Thomas Putnam and his wife.

Judge Danforth The deputy governor of Massachusetts and the presiding judge at the witch trials. Honest and scrupulous, at least in his own mind, Danforth is convinced that he is doing right in rooting out witchcraft.

Giles Corey An elderly but feisty farmer in Salem, famous for his tendency to file lawsuits. Giles's wife, Martha, is accused of witchcraft, and he himself is eventually held in contempt of court and pressed to death with large stones.

Thomas Putnam A wealthy, influential citizen of Salem, Putnam holds a grudge against Francis Nurse for preventing Putnam's brother-in-law from being elected to the office of minister. He uses the witch trials to increase his own wealth by accusing people of witchcraft and then buying up their land.

Ann Putnam Thomas Putnam's wife. Ann Putnam has given birth to eight children, but only Ruth Putnam survived. The other seven died before they were a day old, and Ann is convinced that they were murdered by supernatural means.

Ruth Putnam The Putnams' lone surviving child out of eight. Like Betty Parris, Ruth falls into a strange stupor after Reverend Parris catches her and the other girls dancing in the woods at night.

Tituba Reverend Parris's black slave from Barbados. Tituba agrees to perform voodoo at Abigail's request.

Mary Warren The servant in Thomas Putman's household and a member of Abigail's group of girls. She is a timid girl, easily influenced by those around her, who tried unsuccessfully to expose the hoax and ultimately recanted her confession.

Betty Parris Reverend Parris's ten-year-old daughter. Betty falls into a strange stupor after Parris catches her and the other girls dancing in the forest with Tituba. Her illness and that of Ruth Putnam fuel the first rumors of witchcraft.

Martha Corey Giles Corey's third wife. Martha's reading habits lead to her arrest and conviction for witchcraft.

Ezekiel Cheever A man from Salem who acts as clerk of the court during the witch trials. He is upright and determined to do his duty for justice.

Judge Hathorne A judge who presides, along with Danforth, over the witch trials.

Herrick The marshal of Salem.

Mercy Lewis One of the girls in Abigail's group.

Analysis of Major Characters

John Proctor

In a sense, *The Crucible* has the structure of a classical tragedy, with John Proctor as the play's tragic hero. Honest, upright, and blunt-spoken, Proctor is a good man, but one with a secret, fatal flaw. His lust for Abigail Williams led to their affair (which occurs before the play begins), and created Abigail's jealousy of his wife, Elizabeth, which sets the entire witch hysteria in motion. Once the trials begin, Proctor realizes that he can stop Abigail's rampage through Salem but only if he confesses to his adultery. Such an admission would ruin his good name, and Proctor is, above all, a proud man who places great emphasis on his reputation. He eventually makes an attempt, through Mary Warren's testimony, to name Abigail as a fraud without revealing the crucial information. When this attempt fails, he finally bursts out with a confession, calling Abigail a "whore" and proclaiming his guilt publicly. Only then does he realize that it is too late, that matters have gone too far, and that not even the truth can break the powerful frenzy that he has allowed Abigail to whip up. Proctor's confession succeeds only in leading to *his* arrest and conviction as a witch, and though he lambastes the court and its proceedings, he is also aware of his terrible role in allowing this fervor to grow unchecked.

Proctor redeems himself and provides a final denunciation of the witch trials in his final act. Offered the opportunity to make a public confession of his guilt and live, he almost succumbs, even signing a written confession. His immense pride and fear of public opinion compelled him to withhold his adultery from the court, but by the end of the play he is more concerned with his personal integrity than his public reputation. He still wants to save his name, but for personal and religious, rather than public, reasons. Proctor's refusal to provide a false confession is a true religious and personal stand. Such a confession would dishonor his fellow prisoners, who are brave enough to die as testimony to the truth. Perhaps more relevantly, a false admission would also dishonor him, staining not just his public reputation, but also his soul. By refusing to give up his personal integrity Proctor implicitly proclaims his conviction that such integrity will bring him to heaven. He goes to the gallows redeemed for his earlier sins. As Elizabeth says to end the play, responding to Hale's plea that she convince Proctor to publicly confess: "He have his goodness now. God forbid I take it from him!"

ABIGAIL WILLIAMS

Of the major characters, Abigail is the least complex. She is clearly the villain of the play, more so than Parris or Danforth: she tells lies, manipulates her friends and the entire town, and eventually sends nineteen innocent people to their deaths. Throughout the hysteria, Abigail's motivations never seem more complex than simple jealousy and a desire to have revenge on Elizabeth Proctor. The language of the play is almost biblical, and Abigail seems like a biblical character—a Jezebel figure, driven only by sexual desire and a lust for power. Nevertheless, it is worth pointing out a few background details that, though they don't mitigate Abigail's guilt, make her actions more understandable.

Abigail is an orphan and an unmarried girl; she thus occupies a low rung on the Puritan Salem social ladder (the only people below her are the slaves, like Tituba, and social outcasts). For young girls in Salem, the minister and the other male adults are God's earthly representatives, their authority derived from on high. The trials, then, in which the girls are allowed to act as though they have a direct connection to God, empower the previously powerless Abigail. Once shunned and scorned by the respectable townsfolk who had heard rumors of her affair with John Proctor, Abigail now finds that she has clout, and she takes full advantage of it. A mere accusation from one of Abigail's troop is enough to incarcerate and convict even the most well-respected inhabitant of Salem. Whereas others once reproached her for her adultery, she now has the opportunity to accuse them of the worst sin of all: devil-worship.

REVEREND HALE

John Hale, the intellectual, naïve witch-hunter, enters the play in Act I when Parris summons him to examine his daughter, Betty. In an extended commentary on Hale in Act I, Miller describes him as "a tight-skinned, eager-eyed intellectual. This is a beloved errand for him; on being called here to ascertain witchcraft he has felt the pride of the specialist whose unique knowledge has at last been publicly called for." Hale enters in a flurry of activity, carrying large books and projecting an air of great knowledge. In the early going, he is the force behind the witch trials, probing for confessions and encouraging people to testify. Over the course of the play, however, he experiences a transformation, one more remarkable than that of any other character. Listening to John Proctor and Mary Warren, he becomes convinced that they, not Abigail, are telling the truth. In the climactic scene in the court in Act III, he throws his lot in with those opposing the witch trials. In tragic fashion, his about-face comes too late—the trials are no longer in his hands but rather in those of Danforth and the theocracy, which has no interest in seeing its proceedings exposed as a sham.

The failure of his attempts to turn the tide renders the once-confident Hale a broken man. As his belief in witchcraft falters, so does his faith in the law. In Act IV, it is he who counsels the accused witches to lie, to confess their supposed sins in order to save their own lives. In his change of heart and subsequent despair, Hale gains the audience's sympathy but not its respect, since he lacks the moral fiber of Rebecca Nurse or, as it turns out, John Proctor. Although Hale recognizes the evil of the witch trials, his response is not defiance but surrender. He insists that survival is the highest good, even if it means accommodating oneself to injustice—something that the truly heroic characters can never accept.

THEMES, MOTIFS & SYMBOLS

THEMES

Themes are the fundamental and often universal ideas explored in a literary work.

INTOLERANCE

The Crucible is set in a theocratic society, in which the church and the state are one, and the religion is a strict, austere form of Protestantism known as Puritanism. Because of the theocratic nature of the society, moral laws and state laws are one and the same: sin and the status of an individual's soul are matters of public concern. There is no room for deviation from social norms, since any individual whose private life doesn't conform to the established moral laws represents a threat not only to the public good but also to the rule of God and true religion. In Salem, everything and everyone belongs to either God or the devil; dissent is not merely unlawful, it is associated with satanic activity. This dichotomy functions as the underlying logic behind the witch trials. As Danforth says in Act III, "a person is either with this court or he must be counted against it." The witch trials are the ultimate expression of intolerance (and hanging witches is the ultimate means of restoring the community's purity); the trials brand all social deviants with the taint of devil-worship and thus necessitate their elimination from the community.

HYSTERIA

Another critical theme in *The Crucible* is the role that hysteria can play in tearing apart a community. Hysteria supplants logic and enables people to believe that their neighbors, whom they have always considered upstanding people, are committing absurd and unbelievable crimes—communing with the devil, killing babies, and so on. In *The Crucible,* the townsfolk accept and become active in the hysterical climate not only out of genuine religious piety but also because it gives them a chance to express repressed sentiments and to act on long-held grudges. The most obvious case is Abigail, who uses the situation to accuse Elizabeth Proctor of witchcraft and have her sent to jail. But others thrive on the hysteria as well: Reverend Parris strengthens his position within the village, albeit temporarily, by making scapegoats of people like Proctor who question his authority. The wealthy, ambitious Thomas Putnam gains revenge on Francis Nurse by getting Rebecca, Francis's virtuous wife, convicted of the supernatural murders of Ann Putnam's babies. In the end, hysteria can thrive only because people benefit from it. It suspends the rules of daily life and allows the acting out of every dark desire and hateful urge under the cover of righteousness.

REPUTATION

Reputation is tremendously important in theocratic Salem, where public and private moralities are one and the same. In an environment where reputation plays such an important role, the fear of guilt by association becomes particularly pernicious. Focused on maintaining public reputation, the townsfolk of Salem must fear that the sins of their friends and associates will taint their names. Various characters base their actions on the desire to protect their respective reputations. As the play begins, Parris fears that Abigail's increasingly questionable actions, and the hints of witchcraft surrounding his daughter's coma, will threaten his reputation and force him from the pulpit. Meanwhile, the protagonist, John Proctor, also seeks to keep his good name from being tarnished. Early in the play, he has a chance to put a stop to the girls' accusations, but his desire to preserve his reputation keeps him from testifying against Abigail. At the end of the play, however, Proctor's desire to keep his good name leads him to make the heroic choice not to make a false confession and to go to his death without signing his name to an untrue statement. "I have given you my soul; leave me my name!" he cries to Danforth in Act IV. By refusing to relinquish his name, he redeems himself for his earlier failure and dies with integrity.

THEMES

MOTIFS

Motifs are recurring structures, contrasts, and literary devices that can help to develop and inform the text's major themes.

EMPOWERMENT

The witch trials empower several characters in the play who are previously marginalized in Salem society. In general, women occupy the lowest rung of male-dominated Salem and have few options in life. They work as servants for townsmen until they are old enough to be married off and have children of their own. In addition to being thus restricted, Abigail is also slave to John Proctor's sexual whims—he strips away her innocence when he commits adultery with her, and he arouses her spiteful jealousy when he terminates their affair. Because the Puritans' greatest fear is the defiance of God, Abigail's accusations of witchcraft and devil-worship immediately command the attention of the court. By aligning herself, in the eyes of others, with God's will, she gains power over society, as do the other girls in her pack, and her word becomes virtually unassailable, as do theirs. Tituba, whose status is lower than that of anyone else in the play by virtue of the fact that she is black, manages similarly to deflect blame from herself by accusing others.

ACCUSATIONS, CONFESSIONS, AND LEGAL PROCEEDINGS

The witch trials are central to the action of *The Crucible,* and dramatic accusations and confessions fill the play even beyond the confines of the courtroom. In the first act, even before the hysteria begins, we see Parris accuse Abigail of dishonoring him, and he then makes a series of accusations against his parishioners. Giles Corey and Proctor respond in kind, and Putnam soon joins in, creating a chorus of indictments even before Hale arrives. The entire witch trial system thrives on accusations, the only way that witches can be identified, and confessions, which provide the proof of the justice of the court proceedings. Proctor attempts to break this cycle with a confession of his own, when he admits to the affair with Abigail, but this confession is trumped by the accusation of witchcraft against him, which in turn demands a confession. Proctor's courageous decision, at the close of the play, to die rather than confess to a sin that he did not commit, finally breaks the cycle. The court collapses shortly afterward, undone by the refusal of its victims to propagate lies.

SYMBOLS

Symbols are objects, characters, figures, and colors used to represent abstract ideas or concepts.

THE WITCH TRIALS AND MCCARTHYISM

There is little symbolism within *The Crucible,* but, in its entirety, the play can be seen as symbolic of the paranoia about communism that pervaded America in the 1950s. Several parallels exist between the House Un-American Activities Committee's rooting out of suspected communists during this time and the seventeenth-century witch-hunt that Miller depicts in *The Crucible,* including the narrow-mindedness, excessive zeal, and disregard for the individuals that characterize the government's effort to stamp out a perceived social ill. Further, as with the alleged witches of Salem, suspected Communists were encouraged to confess their crimes and to "name names," identifying others sympathetic to their radical cause. Some have criticized Miller for oversimplifying matters, in that while there were (as far as we know) no actual witches in Salem, there were certainly Communists in 1950s America. However, one can argue that Miller's concern in *The Crucible* is not with whether the accused actually are witches, but rather with the unwillingness of the court officials to believe that they are not. In light of McCarthyist excesses, which wronged many innocents, this parallel was felt strongly in Miller's own time.

SUMMARY & ANALYSIS

ACT I: OPENING SCENE TO THE ENTRANCE OF JOHN PROCTOR

SUMMARY

The play is set in Salem, Massachusetts, 1692; the government is a theocracy—rule by God through religious officials. Hard work and church consume the majority of a Salem resident's time. Within the community, there are simmering disputes over land. Matters of boundaries and deeds are a source of constant, bitter disagreements.

As the play opens, Reverend Parris kneels in prayer in front of his daughter's bed. Ten-year-old Betty Parris lies in an unmoving, unresponsive state. Parris is a grim, stern man suffering from paranoia. He believes that the members of his congregation should not lift a finger during religious services without his permission. The rumor that Betty is the victim of witchcraft is running rampant in Salem, and a crowd has gathered in Parris's parlor. Parris has sent for Reverend John Hale of Beverly, an expert on witchcraft, to determine whether Betty is indeed bewitched. Parris berates his niece, Abigail Williams, because he discovered her, Betty, and several other girls dancing in the forest in the middle of the night with his slave, Tituba. Tituba was intoning unintelligible words and waving her arms over a fire, and Parris thought he spotted someone running naked through the trees.

Abigail denies that she and the girls engaged in witchcraft. She states that Betty merely fainted from shock when her father caught them dancing. Parris fears that his enemies will use the scandal to drive him out of his ministerial office. He asks Abigail if her name and reputation are truly unimpeachable. Elizabeth Proctor, a local woman who once employed Abigail at her home but subsequently fired her, has stopped attending church regularly. There are rumors that Elizabeth does not want to sit so close to a soiled woman. Abigail denies any wrongdoing and asserts that Elizabeth hates her because she would not work like a slave. Parris asks why no other family has hired Abigail if Elizabeth is a liar. Abigail insinuates that Parris is only worried about her employment status because he begrudges her upkeep.

Thomas Putnam and his wife enter the room. Putnam holds one of the play's many simmering grudges. His brother-in-law was a candidate for the Salem ministry, but a small faction thwarted his relative's aspirations. Mrs. Putnam reports that their own daughter, Ruth, is as listless as Betty, and she claims that someone saw Betty flying over a neighbor's barn.

Mrs. Putnam had seven babies that each died within a day of its birth. Convinced that someone used witchcraft to murder them, she sent Ruth to Tituba to contact the spirits of her dead children in order to discover the identity of the murderer. Parris berates Abigail anew and asserts that she and the girls were indeed practicing witchcraft. Putnam urges Parris to head off his enemies and promptly announce that he has discovered witchcraft. Mercy Lewis, the Putnams' servant, drops in and reports that Ruth seems better. Parris agrees to meet the crowd and lead them in a prayer, but he refuses to mention witchcraft until he gets Reverend Hale's opinion.

Once they are alone, Abigail updates Mercy on the current situation. Mary Warren, the servant for the Proctor household, enters the room in a breathless, nervous state. She frets that they will all be labeled witches before long. Betty sits up suddenly and cries for her mother, but her mother is dead and buried. Abigail tells the girls that she has told Parris everything about their activities in the woods, but Betty cries that Abigail did not tell Parris about drinking blood as a charm to kill Elizabeth Proctor, John Proctor's wife. Abigail strikes Betty across the face and warns the other girls to confess *only* that they danced and that Tituba conjured Ruth's dead sisters. She threatens to kill them if they breathe a word about the other things that they did. She shakes Betty, but Betty has returned to her unmoving, unresponsive state.

Analysis

The Crucible is a play about the intersection of private sins with paranoia, hysteria, and religious intolerance. The citizens of Arthur Miller's Salem of 1692 would consider the very concept of a private life heretical. The government of Salem, and of Massachusetts as a whole, is a theocracy, with the legal system based on the Christian Bible. Moral laws and state laws are one and the same; sin and the status of an individual's soul are public concerns. An individual's private life must conform to the moral laws, or the individual represents a threat to the public good.

Regulating the morality of citizens requires surveillance. For every inhabitant of Salem, there is a potential witness to the individual's private crimes. State officials patrol the township, requiring citizens to give an account of their activities. Free speech is not a protected right, and saying the wrong thing can easily land a citizen in jail. Most of the punishments, such as the stocks, whipping, and hangings, are public, with the punishment serving to shame the lawbreaker and remind the public that to disagree with the state's decisions is to disagree with God's will.

The Crucible introduces a community full of underlying personal grudges. Religion pervades every aspect of life, but it is a religion that lacks a ritual outlet to manage emotions such as anger, jealousy, or resentment. By 1692, Salem has become a fairly established community, removed from its days as an outpost on a hostile frontier. Many of the former dangers that united the community in its early years have lessened, while interpersonal feuds and grudges over property, religious offices, and sexual behavior have begun to simmer beneath the theocratic surface. These tensions, combined with the paranoia about supernatural forces, pervade the town's religious sensibility and provide the raw materials for the hysteria of the witch trials.

On the surface, Parris appears to be an anxious, worried father. However, if we pay close attention to his language, we find indications that he is mainly worried about his reputation, not the welfare of his daughter and their friends. He fears that Abigail, Betty, and the other girls were engaging in witchcraft when he caught them dancing, and his first concern is not the endangerment of their souls but the trouble that the scandal will cause him. It is possible—and likely, from his point of view—that members in the community would make use of a moral transgression to ruin him. Parris's anxiety about the insecurity of his office reveals the extent to which conflicts divide the Salem community. Not even those individuals who society believes are invested with God's will can control the whim of the populace.

The idea of guilt by association is central to the events in *The Crucible*, as it is one of the many ways in which the private, moral behavior of citizens can be regulated. An individual must fear that the sins of his or her friends and associates will taint his or her own name. Therefore, the individual is pressured to govern his or her private relationships according to public opinion and public law. To solidify one's good name, it is necessary to publicly condemn the

wrongdoing of others. In this way, guilt by association also rein-
forces the publicization of private sins. Even before the play begins,
Abigail's increasingly questionable reputation, in light of her unex-
plained firing by the upright Elizabeth Proctor, threatens her uncle
Parris's tenuous hold on power and authority in the community.
The allegations of witchcraft only render her an even greater threat
to him.

Putnam, meanwhile, has his own set of grudges against his fellow Salemites. A rich man from an influential Salem family, he believes that his status grants him the right to worldly success. Yet he
has been thwarted, both in his efforts to make his brother-in-law
minister, and in his family life, where his children have all died in
infancy. Putnam is well positioned to use the witch trials to express
his feelings of persecution and undeserved failure, and to satisfy his
need for revenge. His wife feels similarly wronged—like many Puritans, she is all too willing to blame the tragic deaths of her children
on supernatural causes—and seeks similar retribution for what she
perceives as the malevolent doings of others.

ACT I: THE ENTRANCE OF JOHN PROCTOR TO THE ENTRANCE OF REVEREND HALE

SUMMARY

> *I never knew what pretense Salem was, I never knew
> the lying lessons. . . .*
>
> (See QUOTATIONS, *p. 39*)

John Proctor, a local farmer, enters Parris's house to join the girls.
Proctor disdains hypocrisy, and many people resent him for exposing their foolishness. However, Proctor is uneasy with himself because he had conducted an extramarital affair with Abigail. His
wife, Elizabeth, discovered the affair and promptly dismissed Abigail from her work at the Proctor home.

Proctor caustically reminds Mary Warren, who now works for
him, that he forbade her to leave his house, and he threatens to
whip her if she does not obey his rules. Mercy Lewis and Mary
depart. Abigail declares that she waits for Proctor at night. Proctor
angers her by replying that he made no promises to her during
their affair. She retorts that he cannot claim that he has no feelings
for her because she has seen him looking up at her window. He
admits that he still harbors kind feelings for her but asserts that

their relationship is over. Abigail mocks Proctor for bending to the will of his "cold, sniveling" wife. Proctor threatens to give Abigail a whipping for insulting his wife. Abigail cries that Proctor put knowledge in her heart, and she declares that he cannot ask her to forget what she has learned—namely, that all of Salem operates on pretense and lies.

The crowd in the parlor sings a psalm. At the phrase "going up to Jesus," Betty covers her ears and collapses into hysterics. Parris, Mercy, and the Putnams rush into the room. Mrs. Putnam concludes that Betty is bewitched and cannot hear the Lord's name without pain. Rebecca Nurse, an elderly woman, joins them. Her husband, Francis Nurse, is highly respected in Salem, and many people ask him to arbitrate their disputes. Over the years, he gradually bought up the 300 acres that he once rented, and some people resent his success. He and Thomas Putnam bitterly disputed a matter of land boundaries. Moreover, Francis belonged to the faction that prevented Putnam's brother-in-law from winning the Salem ministry. Giles Corey, a muscular, wiry eighty-three-year-old farmer, joins the crowd in the room as Rebecca stands over Betty. Betty gradually quiets in Rebecca's gentle presence. Rebecca assures everyone that Ruth and Betty are probably only suffering from a childish fit, derived from overstimulation.

Proctor asks if Parris consulted the legal authorities or called a town meeting before he asked Reverend Hale to uncover demons in Salem. Rebecca fears that a witch-hunt will spark even more disputes. Putnam demands that Parris have Hale search for signs of witchcraft. Proctor reminds Putnam that he cannot command Parris and states that Salem does not grant votes on the basis of wealth. Putnam retorts that Proctor should not worry about Salem's government because he does not attend church regularly like a good citizen. Proctor announces that he does not agree with Parris's emphasis on "hellfire and damnation" in his sermons.

Parris and Giles bicker over the question of whether Parris should be granted six pounds for firewood expenses. Parris claims that the six pounds are part of his salary and that his contract stipulates that the community provide him with firewood. Giles claims that Parris overstepped his boundaries in asking for the deed to his (Parris's) house. Parris replies that he does not want the community to be able to toss him out on a whim; his possession of the deed will make it more difficult for citizens to disobey the church.

Parris contends that Proctor does not have the right to defy his religious authority. He reminds Proctor that Salem is not a community of Quakers, and he advises Proctor to inform his "followers" of this fact. Parris declares that Proctor belongs to a faction in the church conspiring against him. Proctor shocks everyone when he says that he does not like Parris's kind of authority and would love to find and join this enemy faction.

Putnam and Proctor argue over the proper ownership of a piece of timberland where Proctor harvests his lumber. Putnam claims that his grandfather left the tract of land to him in his will. Proctor says that he purchased the land from Francis Nurse, adding that Putnam's grandfather had a habit of willing land that did not belong to him. Putnam, growing irate, threatens to sue Proctor.

ANALYSIS

In Puritan Salem, young women such as Abigail, Mary, and Mercy are largely powerless until they get married. As a young, unmarried servant girl, Mary is expected to obey the will of her employer, Proctor, who can confine her to his home and even whip her for disobeying his orders.

Proctor, in his first appearance, is presented as a quick-witted, sharp-tongued man with a strong independent streak. These traits would seem to make him a good person to question the motives of those who cry witchcraft. However, his guilt over his affair with Abigail makes his position problematic because he is guilty of the very hypocrisy that he despises in others. Abigail, meanwhile, is clearly not over their affair. She accuses Proctor of "putting knowledge" in her heart. In one sense, Abigail accuses him of destroying her innocence by taking her virginity. In another sense, she also accuses him of showing her the extent to which hypocrisy governs social relations in Salem. Abigail's cynicism about her society reveals that she is well positioned to take advantage of the witch trials for personal gain as well as revenge. Her secret desire to remove Elizabeth Proctor from her path to John Proctor drives the hysteria that soon develops.

Proctor's inquiry as to whether Parris consulted anyone before seeking out Reverend Hale illustrates another constricting aspect of Salem society: the emphasis on public morality and the public good renders individual action suspect. Proctor's question subtly insinuates that Parris has personal, private, motives for calling Reverend Hale. He compounds the tension between the two by hinting that Parris's fire and brimstone sermons further the minister's individual interests by encouraging people to obey him, lest they risk going to hell.

Parris is one of the least appealing characters in the play. Suspicious and grasping, he has a strong attachment to the material side of life. It is obvious that his emphasis on hellfire and damnation is, at least in part, an attempt to coerce the congregation into giving him more material benefits out of guilt. Parris, Miller mentions in an aside to the audience, was once a merchant in Barbados. His commercialist zeal shows in the way he uses sin as a sort of currency to procure free firewood and free houses. He would have his congregation pay God for their sins, but he wants to collect on their debts himself.

Parris's desire to own the deed to his house is likewise telling. He explains his reasons in terms of the community's fickle attitude toward its ministers—in this, at least, he has a point. Before his arrival, the Putnams and the Nurses engaged in a bitter dispute over the choice of minister, a quarrel that offers ample evidence of a minister's vulnerability to political battles and personal grudges between families. However, Parris's claim that he wants only to ensure "obedience to the Church" is suspect, given that he reacts to disagreement with the church's edicts as though it were a personal insult. His allegation that Proctor leads a church faction intent on bringing about his downfall reveals that Parris is fairly paranoid. This paranoia, coupled with his actual political vulnerability, primes him to take advantage of the witch trials to protect his personal interests.

Rebecca's insistence to Proctor that he not "break charity" with the minister suggests that there are few ways to express individual disagreements in Salem because doing so is considered immoral. Feelings of jealousy and resentment have no outlet other than the court, which, in theocratic Salem, is also an institution of religious authority. The entire community of Salem is thus ripe for the witch trials to become an outlet for the expression of economic, political, and personal grudges through the manipulation of religious and moral authority. The land dispute between Proctor and Putnam adds the final touch to the implication that the real issues in the witch trials have much more to do with intra-societal and interpersonal concerns than with supernatural manifestations of the devil's influence.

ACT I: THE ENTRANCE OF REVEREND HALE
TO THE CLOSING SCENE

SUMMARY

> *I saw Sarah Good with the Devil! I saw Goody Osburn*
> *with the Devil! I saw Bridget Bishop with the Devil!*
> *(See* QUOTATIONS, *p. 40)*

Reverend Hale is an intellectual man, and he has studied witchcraft extensively. He arrives at Parris's home with a heavy load of books. Hale asks Proctor and Giles if they have afflicted children. Giles says that Proctor does not believe in witches. Proctor denies having stated an opinion on witches at all and leaves Hale to his work.

Parris relates the tale of finding the girls dancing in the forest at night, and Mrs. Putnam reports having sent her daughter to conjure the spirits of her dead children. She asks if losing seven children before they live a day is a natural occurrence. Hale consults his books while Rebecca announces that she is too old to sit in on the proceedings. Parris insists that they may find the source of all the community's troubles, but she leaves anyway.

Giles asks Hale what reading strange books means because he often finds his wife, Martha, reading books. The night before, he tried to pray but found that he could not succeed until Martha closed her book and left the house. (Giles has a bad reputation in Salem, and people generally blame him for thefts and random fires. He cares little for public opinion, and he only began attending church regularly after he married Martha. Giles does not mention that he only recently learned any prayers and that even small distractions cause him problems in reciting them.) Hale thoughtfully considers the information and concludes that they will have to discuss the matter later. Slightly taken aback, Giles states that he does not mean to say that his wife is a witch. He just wants to know what she reads and why she hides the books from him.

Hale questions Abigail about the dancing in the forest, but Abigail maintains that the dancing was not connected to witchcraft. Parris hesitantly adds that he saw a kettle in the grass when he caught the girls at their dancing. Abigail claims that it contained soup, but Parris insists that he saw something moving in it. Abigail says that a frog jumped in. Under severe questioning, she insists that she did not call the devil but that Tituba did. She denies drinking any of the brew in the kettle, but when the men bring Tituba to the room, Abigail points at her and announces that Tituba made her drink blood. Tituba tells Parris and Hale that Abigail begged her to conjure and concoct a charm.

Tituba insists that someone else is bewitching the children because the devil has many witches in his service. Hale counsels her to open herself to God's glory, and he asks if she has ever seen someone that she knows from Salem with the devil. Putnam suggests Sarah Good or Goody Osburn, two local outcasts. In a rising tide of religious exultation, Tituba says that she saw four people with the devil. She informs Parris that the devil told her many times to kill him in his sleep, but she refused even though the devil promised to grant her freedom and send her back to her native Barbados in return for her obedience. She recounts that the devil told her that he even had white people in his power and that he showed her Sarah Good and Goody Osburn. Mrs. Putnam declares that Tituba's story makes sense because Goody Osburn midwifed three of her ill-fated births. Abigail adds Bridget Bishop's name to the list of the accused. Betty rises from the bed and chants more names. The scene closes as Abigail and Betty, in feverish ecstasy, alternate in piling up names on the growing list. Hale calls for the marshal to bring irons to arrest the accused witches.

ANALYSIS

In a theocracy, part of the state's role is policing belief. Therefore, there is a good deal of pressure on the average citizen to inform on the blasphemous speech of his or her neighbors in the name of Christian duty. Giles's claim to Hale that Proctor does not believe in witches does not necessarily arise out of a desire to do his Christian duty—he may only be making a joke. However, the very offhand nature of his statement indicates that reporting a neighbor's heretical words or thoughts is a deeply ingrained behavior in Salem.

Rebecca, a figure of respectability and good sense, fears that an investigation into witchcraft will only increase division within the Salem community. Parris's declaration that a thorough investigation could get at the root of all the community's problems proves accurate, though not in the way that he foresees. The witch trials do bring out all of the community's problems, but in the worst possible way. The specter of witchcraft allows citizens to blame political failures, the deaths of children, and land squabbles on supernatural influences. No one has to accept individual responsibility for any of the conflicts that divide the community or confront any of his or her personal issues with other individuals because everyone can simply say, "The devil made me do it."

Reverend Hale's reaction to Giles's story about Martha reveals the dangerous implications of a zealous witch-hunt. Ordinarily, reading books not related to the Bible would be considered an immoral use of one's time, but it certainly would not be interpreted as evidence of witchcraft. But with Hale present and the scent of witchcraft in the air, the slightest unorthodox behavior automatically makes someone suspect.

Abigail's reaction to the mounting pressure determines the way in which the rest of the witch trials will play out. Because she can no longer truly deny her involvement in witchcraft, she accepts her guilt but displaces it onto Tituba. She admits being involved in witchcraft but declares that Tituba forced her into it. Tituba's reaction to being accused follows Abigail's lead: she admits her guilt in a public setting and receives absolution and then completes her self-cleansing by passing her guilt on to others. In this manner, the admission of involvement with witchcraft functions like the ritual of confession.

The ritual of confession in the witch trials also allows the expression of sentiments that could not otherwise be verbalized in repressive Salem. By placing her own thoughts in the devil's mouth, Tituba can express her long-held aggression against the man who enslaves her. Moreover, she states that the devil tempted her by showing her some white people that he owned. By naming the devil as a slave owner, she subtly accuses Parris and other white citizens of doing the devil's work in condoning slavery. Tituba is normally a powerless figure; in the context of the witch trials, however, she gains a power and authority previously unknown to her. No one would have listened seriously to a word she had to say before, but she now has a position of authority from which to name the secret sins of other Salem residents. She uses that power and authority to make accusations that would have earned her a beating before. The girls—Abigail and Betty—follow the same pattern, empowering themselves through their allegedly religious hysteria.

Act II

Summary

John Proctor sits down to dinner with his wife, Elizabeth. Mary Warren, their servant, has gone to the witch trials, defying Elizabeth's order that she remain in the house. Fourteen people are now in jail. If these accused witches do not confess, they will be hanged. Whoever Abigail and her troop name as they go into hysterics is arrested for bewitching the girls.

Proctor can barely believe the craze, and he tells Elizabeth that Abigail had sworn her dancing had nothing to do with witchcraft. Elizabeth wants him to testify that the accusations are a sham. He says that he cannot prove his allegation because Abigail told him this information while they were alone in a room. Elizabeth loses all faith in her husband upon hearing that he and Abigail were alone together. Proctor demands that she stop judging him. He says that he feels as though his home is a courtroom, but Elizabeth responds that the real court is in his own heart.

When Mary Warren returns home, she gives Elizabeth a doll that she sewed in court, saying that it is a gift. She reports that thirty-nine people now stand accused. John and Mary argue over whether Mary can continue attending the trials. He threatens to whip her, and Mary declares that she saved Elizabeth's life that day. Elizabeth's name was apparently mentioned in the accusations (Mary will not name the accuser), but Mary spoke out in Elizabeth's defense. Proctor instructs Mary to go to bed, but she demands that he stop ordering her around. Elizabeth, meanwhile, is convinced that it was Abigail who accused her of witchcraft, in order to take her place in John's bed.

Hale visits the Proctors because he wants to speak with everyone whose name has been mentioned in connection with witchcraft. He has just visited Rebecca Nurse. Hale proceeds to ask questions about the Christian character of the Proctor home. He notes that the Proctors have not often attended church and that their youngest son is not yet baptized. Proctor explains that he does not like Parris's particular theology. Hale asks them to recite the Ten Commandments. Proctor obliges but forgets the commandment prohibiting adultery.

At Elizabeth's urging, Proctor informs Hale that Abigail told him that the children's sickness had nothing to do with witchcraft. Taken aback, Hale replies that many have already confessed. Proctor points out that they would have been hanged without a confession. Giles and Francis rush into Proctor's home, crying that their wives have been arrested. Rebecca is charged with the supernatural murders of Mrs. Putnam's babies. A man bought a pig from Martha Corey and it died not long afterward; he wanted his money back, but she refused, saying that he did not know how to care for a pig. Every pig he purchased thereafter died, and he accused her of bewitching him so that he would be incapable of keeping one alive.

Ezekiel Cheever and Herrick, the town marshal, arrive with a warrant for Elizabeth's arrest. Hale is surprised because, last he heard, Elizabeth was not charged with anything. Cheever asks if Elizabeth owns any dolls, and Elizabeth replies that she has not owned dolls since she was a girl. Cheever spies the doll Mary Warren gave her. He finds a needle inside it. Cheever relates that Abigail had a fit at dinner in Parris's house that evening. Parris found a needle in her abdomen, and Abigail accused Elizabeth of witchcraft. Elizabeth brings Mary downstairs. Mary informs the inquisitors that she made the doll while in court and stuck the needle in it herself.

As Elizabeth is led away, Proctor loses his temper and rips the warrant. He asks Hale why the accuser is always considered innocent. Hale appears less and less certain of the accusations of witchcraft. Proctor tells Mary that she has to testify in court that she made the doll and put the needle in it. Mary declares that Abigail will kill her if she does and that Abigail would only charge him with lechery. Proctor is shocked that Abigail told Mary about the affair, but he demands that she testify anyway. Mary cries hysterically that she cannot.

ANALYSIS

Abigail and her troop have achieved an extremely unusual level of power and authority for young, unmarried girls in a Puritan community. They can destroy the lives of others with a mere accusation, and even the wealthy and influential are not safe. Mary Warren is so full of her newfound power that she feels able to defy Proctor's assumption of authority over her. She invokes her own power as an official of the court, a power that Proctor cannot easily deny.

Proctor's sense of guilt begins to eat away at him. He knows that he can bring down Abigail and end her reign of terror, but he fears for his good name if his hidden sin of adultery is revealed. The pressing knowledge of his own guilt makes him feel judged, but Elizabeth is correct when she points out that the judge who pursues him so mercilessly is himself. Proctor has a great loathing for hypocrisy, and, here, he judges his own hypocrisy no less harshly than that of others.

Proctor's intense dilemma over whether to expose his own sin to bring down Abigail is complicated by Hale's decision to visit everyone whose name is even remotely associated with the accusations of witchcraft. Hale wants to determine the character of each accused individual by measuring it against Christian standards. His invasion of the home space in the name of God reveals the essential nature of the trials—namely, to root out hidden sins and expose them. Any small deviation from doctrine is reason for suspicion. Proctor tries to prove the upright character of his home by reciting the Ten Commandments. In forgetting to name adultery, however, just as he "forgot" it during his affair with Abigail, he not only exposes the deficiency of his Christian morality but also suggests the possibility that his entire household has succumbed to the evil influence of the devil and witchcraft.

When Proctor asks indignantly why the accusers are always automatically innocent, he comments upon the essential attractiveness of taking the side of the accusers. Many of the accusations have come through the ritual confession of guilt—one confesses guilt and then proves one's "innocence" by accusing others. The accusing side enjoys a privileged position of moral virtue from this standpoint. Proctor laments the lack of hard evidence, but, of course (as Danforth will later point out), in supernatural crimes, the standards of evidence are not as hard and fast. The only "proof" is the word of the alleged victims of witchcraft. Thus, to deny these victims' charges is almost a denial of the existence of witchcraft itself—quite a heretical claim. Therefore, those who take the side of the accusers can enjoy the self-justifying mission of doing God's will in rooting out the devil's work, while those who challenge them are threatening the very foundations of Salem society.

Hale, meanwhile, is undergoing an internal crisis. He clearly enjoyed being called to Salem because it made him feel like an expert. His pleasure in the trials comes from his privileged position of authority with respect to defining the guilty and the innocent. However, his surprise at hearing of Rebecca's arrest and the warrant for Elizabeth's arrest reveals that Hale is no longer in control of the proceedings. Power has passed into the hands of others, and as the craze spreads, Hale begins to doubt its essential justice.

Act III

Summary

> [A] person is either with this court or he must be
> counted against it, there be no road between.
>
> (See QUOTATIONS, p. 41)

Back in Salem, the court is in session. Giles interrupts the proceedings by shouting that Putnam is only making a grab for more land. He claims to have evidence to back up this assertion. Judge Hathorne, Deputy Governor Danforth, and the Reverends Hale and Parris join Giles and Francis in the vestry room to get to the bottom of the matter. Proctor and Mary Warren enter the room. Mary testifies that she and the other girls were only pretending to be afflicted by witchcraft. Judge Danforth, shocked, asks Proctor if he has told the village about Mary's claims. Parris declares that they all want to overthrow the court.

Danforth asks Proctor if he is attempting to undermine the court. Proctor assures him that he just wants to free his wife, but Cheever informs the judge that Proctor ripped up the warrant for Elizabeth's arrest. Danforth proceeds to question Proctor about his religious beliefs. He is particularly intrigued by the information, offered by Parris, that Proctor only attends church about once a month. Cheever adds that Proctor plows on Sunday, a serious offense in Salem.

Danforth and Hathorne inform Proctor that he need not worry about Elizabeth's imminent execution because she claims to be pregnant. She will not be hanged until after she delivers. Danforth asks if he will drop his condemnation of the court, but Proctor refuses. He submits a deposition signed by ninety-one land-owning farmers attesting to the good characters of Elizabeth, Martha, and Rebecca. Parris insists that they all be summoned for questioning because the deposition is an attack on the court. Hale asks why every defense is considered an attack on the court.

Putnam is led into the room to answer to an allegation by Giles that he prompted his daughter to accuse George Jacobs of witchcraft. Should Jacobs hang, he would forfeit his property, and Putnam is the only person in Salem with the money to purchase such a tract. Giles refuses to name the man who gave him the information because he does not want to open him to Putnam's vengeance. Danforth arrests Giles for contempt of court.

Danforth sends for Abigail and her troop of girls. Abigail denies Mary's testimony, as well as her explanation for the doll in the Proctor home. Mary maintains her assertion that the girls are only pretending. Hathorne asks her to pretend to faint for them. Mary says she cannot because she does not have "the sense of it" now. Under continued pressure, she falters and explains that she only thought she saw spirits. Danforth pressures Abigail to be truthful. Abigail shivers and the other girls follow suit. They accuse Mary of bewitching them with a cold wind.

Proctor leaps at Abigail and calls her a whore. He confesses his affair with her and explains that Elizabeth fired her when she discovered it. He claims that Abigail wants Elizabeth to hang so that she can take her place in his home. Danforth orders Abigail and Proctor to turn their backs, and he sends for Elizabeth, who is reputed by Proctor to be unfailingly honest. Danforth asks why she fired Abigail. Elizabeth glances at Proctor for a clue, but Danforth demands that she look only at him while she speaks. Elizabeth claims to have gotten the mistaken notion that Proctor fancied Abigail, so she lost her temper and fired the girl without just cause. As marshal, Herrick removes Elizabeth from the room. Proctor cries out that he confessed his sin, but it is too late for Elizabeth to change her story. Hale begs Danforth to reconsider, stating that Abigail has always struck him as false.

Abigail and the girls begin screaming that Mary is sending her spirit at them. Mary pleads with them to stop, but the girls repeat her words verbatim. The room erupts into a hectic frenzy of fear, excitement, and confusion. Mary seems to become infected with the hysteria of the other girls and starts screaming too. Proctor tries to touch her, but she dashes away from him, calling him the devil's man. She accuses him of consorting with the devil and pressuring her to join him in his evil ways. Danforth orders Proctor's arrest against Hale's vocal opposition. Hale denounces the proceedings and declares that he is quitting the court.

> [I]t is a whore's vengeance. . . .
> (See QUOTATIONS, p. 42)

ANALYSIS

The desperate attempt by Giles, Proctor, and Francis to save their respective wives exposes the extent to which the trials have become about specific individuals and institutions struggling to maintain power and authority. Deputy Governor Danforth and Judge Ha-thorne do not want to admit publicly that they were deceived by a bunch of young women and girls, while Parris does not want the trials to end as a fraud because the scandal of having a lying daughter and niece would end his career in Salem. Predictably, the judge and the deputy governor react to Proctor's claims by accusing him of trying to undermine "the court," which, in theocratic Salem, is tantamount to undermining God himself.

In order to dispose of Proctor's threat, Danforth and Hathorne exercise their power to invade his privacy. Although Proctor has not yet been formally accused of witchcraft, Danforth and Hathorne, like Hale earlier, question him about his Christian morals as though he were already on trial. They hope to find in his character even the slightest deviation from Christian doctrine because they would then be able to cast him as an enemy of religion. Once thus labeled, Proctor would have virtually no chance of anyone in God-fearing Salem intervening on his behalf.

The reaction of Danforth and Hathorne to the deposition signed by ninety-one land-owning citizens further demonstrates the power of the court to invade the private lives of citizens, and indicates the extent to which the court believes in guilt by association. In the witch trials, guilt need not be proven by hard evidence, and signing a deposition attesting to the good character of the accused is enough to put oneself under the same suspicion of guilt. Over the protests of Francis, Danforth states that the signers should have nothing to worry about if they are innocent. The desire for privacy becomes an automatic sign of guilt. Revealingly, Parris states that the goal of the trials is to find precisely what is not seen—in both the supernatural realm and the realm of people's private lives.

During a bout of hysteria such as the witch trials, authority and power fall to those who can avoid questioning while forcing others to speak. By virtue of their rank, Danforth and Hathorne have the authority to cast any questions put to them as an attack on the court. Similarly, Abigail responds to Proctor's charges of harlotry with a refusal to answer questions. Although Danforth's patience with her presumptuous manner is limited, the fact that a young girl can so indignantly refuse to answer a direct question from a court official indicates that she possesses an unusual level of authority for her age and gender.

Much of Act III has to do with determining who will define innocence and guilt. Proctor makes one desperate bid for this authority by finally overcoming his desire to protect his good name, exposing his own secret sin. He hopes to replace his wife's alleged guilt with his own guilt and bring down Abigail in the process. Unfortunately, he mistakes the proceedings for an actual search for the guilty, when, in fact, the proceedings are better described as a power struggle. He exposes his private life to scrutiny, hoping to gain some authority, but he does not realize that too many influential people have invested energy into the proceedings for him to be able to stop them now. Too many reputations are at stake, and Proctor's revelation comes too late to stop the avalanche.

Act IV–Epilogue

Summary: Act IV

> *How may I live without my name? I have given you my soul; leave me my name!*
>
> *(See* quotations, *p. 43)*

That fall, Danforth and Hathorne visit a Salem jail to see Parris. Parris, worn and gaunt, greets them. They demand to know why Reverend Hale has returned to Salem. Parris assures them that Hale only wants to persuade the holdout prisoners to confess and save themselves from the gallows. He reports that Abigail and Mercy vanished from Salem after robbing him. Hale now appears, haggard and sorrowful. He begs the men to pardon the prisoners because the prisoners will not confess. Danforth replies that postponement or pardons will cast doubt not only on the guilt of the seven remaining prisoners but also on that of the twelve who have hanged already. Hale warns that the officials are courting rebellion. As a result of the trials, cows are wandering loose, crops are rotting in the fields, and orphans are wandering without supervision. Many homes have fallen into neglect because their owners were in jail or had to attend the proceedings. Everyone lives in fear of being accused of witchcraft, and there are rumors of revolt in nearby Andover.

Hale has not yet spoken to Proctor. Danforth hopes that Elizabeth can persuade him to confess. Elizabeth agrees to speak with Proctor, but she makes no promises. Everyone leaves the room to allow Elizabeth and Proctor privacy. Elizabeth tells Proctor that almost one hundred people have confessed to witchcraft. She relates that Giles was killed by being pressed to death by large stones, though he never pleaded guilty or not guilty to the charges against him. Had he denied the charges, the court would have hanged him, and he would have forfeited his property. He decided not to enter a plea, so that his farm would fall to his sons. In order to force him to enter a plea, the court tortured him on the press, but he continually refused, and the weight on his chest eventually became so great that it crushed him. His last words were "more weight."

Proctor asks Elizabeth if she thinks that he should confess. He says that he does not hold out, like Rebecca and Martha, because of religious conviction. Rather, he does so out of spite because he wants his persecutors to feel the weight of guilt for seeing him hanged when they know he is innocent.

After wrestling with his conscience for a long time, Proctor agrees to confess. Hathorne and Danforth are overjoyed and Cheever grabs paper, pen, and ink to write the confession. Proctor asks why it has to be written. Danforth informs him that it will be hung on the church door.

The men bring Rebecca to witness Proctor's confession, hoping that she will follow his example. The sight of Rebecca shames Proctor. He offers his confession, and Danforth asks him if he ever saw Rebecca Nurse in the devil's company. Proctor states that he did not. Danforth reads the names of the condemned out loud and asks if he ever saw any of them with the devil. Proctor again replies in the negative. Danforth pressures him to name other guilty parties, but Proctor declares that he will speak only about his own sins.

Proctor hesitates to sign the confession, saying that it is enough that the men have witnessed him admitting his alleged crimes. Under pressure, he signs his name but snatches the sheet from Danforth. Danforth demands the confession as proof to the village of Proctor's witchcraft. Proctor refuses to allow him to nail the paper with his name on the church door and, after arguing with the magistrates, tears the confession in two and renounces it. Danforth calls for the marshal. Herrick leads the seven condemned prisoners, including Proctor, to the gallows. Hale and Parris plead with Elizabeth to remonstrate with Proctor, but she refuses to sway him from doing what he believes is just.

Summary: Epilogue
Not long afterward, Parris is voted out of office. He leaves Salem, never to be heard from again. Rumors have it that Abigail became

a prostitute in Boston. Elizabeth remarries a few years after her husband's execution. In 1712, the excommunications of the condemned are retracted. The farms of the executed go fallow and remain vacant for years.

ANALYSIS

Months have passed, and things are falling apart in Massachusetts, making Danforth and Hathorne increasingly insecure. They do not want to, and ultimately cannot, admit that they made a mistake in signing the death warrants of the nineteen convicted, so they hope for confessions from the remaining prisoners to insulate them from accusations of mistaken verdicts. Danforth cannot pardon the prisoners, despite Hale's pleas and his obvious doubts about their guilt, because he does not want to "cast doubt" on the justification of the hangings of the twelve previously condemned and on the sentence of hanging for the seven remaining prisoners. In the twisted logic of the court, it would not be "fair" to the twelve already hanged if the seven remaining prisoners were pardoned. Danforth prioritizes a bizarre, abstract notion of equality over the tangible reality of potential innocence.

Clearly, the most important issue for the officials of the court is the preservation of their reputations and the integrity of the court. As a theocratic institution, the court represents divine, as well as secular, justice. To admit to twelve mistaken hangings would be to question divine justice and the very foundations of the state and of human life. The integrity of the court would be shattered, and the reputations of court officials would fall with it. Danforth and Hathorne would rather preserve the appearance of justice than threaten the religious and political order of Salem.

Danforth and Hathorne's treatment of Proctor reveals an obsessive need to preserve the appearance of order and justify their actions as well as a hypocritical attitude about honesty. They want Proctor to sign a confession that admits his own status as a witch, testifies to the effect that he saw the other six prisoners in the company of the devil, and completely corroborates the court's findings. While they seek to take advantage of Proctor's reputation for honesty in order to support their claims of having conducted themselves justly, Danforth and Hathorne are wholly unwilling to believe Proctor when he says that he has conducted himself justly.

Proctor's refusal to take part in the ritual transfer of guilt that has dominated the play—the naming of other "witches"—separates him from the rest of the accused. His unwillingness to sign his name to the confession results in part from his desire not to dishonor his fellow prisoners' decisions to stand firm. More important, however, Proctor fixates on his name and on how it will be destroyed if he signs the confession. Proctor's desire to preserve his good name earlier keeps him from testifying against Abigail, leading to disastrous consequences. Now, however, he has finally come to a true understanding of what a good reputation means, and his defense of his name, in the form of not signing the confession, enables him to muster the courage to die heroically. His goodness and honesty, lost during his affair with Abigail, are recovered.

IMPORTANT QUOTATIONS EXPLAINED

1. I look for John Proctor that took me from my sleep and put
    knowledge in my heart! I never knew what pretense Salem
    was, I never knew the lying lessons I was taught by all these
    Christian women and their covenanted men! And now you
    bid me tear the light out of my eyes? I will not, I cannot!
    You loved me, John Proctor, and whatever sin it is, you
    love me yet!

Abigail Williams utters these words in an Act I conversation with
John Proctor, clueing the audience in to her past affair with him.
For Proctor, we quickly realize, their relationship belongs to the
past—while he may still be attracted to her, he is desperately trying
to put the incident behind him. Abigail, on the other hand, has no
such sense of closure, as this quote makes clear. As she begs him to
come back to her, her anger overflows, and we see the roots of what
becomes her targeted, destructive romp through Salem. First, there
is her jealousy of Elizabeth Proctor and her fantasy that if she could
only dispose of Elizabeth, John would be hers. But second, and perhaps more important, we see in this quotation a fierce loathing of
the entire town—"I never knew what pretense Salem was, I never
knew the lying lessons. . . ." Abigail hates Salem, and in the course
of *The Crucible,* she makes Salem pay.

2.   I want to open myself! . . . I want the light of God, I want
the sweet love of Jesus! I danced for the Devil; I saw him, I
wrote in his book; I go back to Jesus; I kiss His hand. I saw
Sarah Good with the Devil! I saw Goody Osburn with the
Devil! I saw Bridget Bishop with the Devil!

This outburst from Abigail comes at the end of Act I, after the slave-
girl Tituba has confessed to witchcraft. Abigail spent the first act
worrying desperately about the possibility of being disgraced for
having cast charms with her friends in the forest. Tituba's confession, however, offers an example of a way out, and Abigail takes
it. She "confesses" to consorting with the Devil, which, according
to the theology of Salem, means that she is redeemed and free from
guilt. Then, as the next step in absolving herself of sin, she accuses
others of being witches, thus shifting the burden of shame from her
shoulders to those she names. Seeing Abigail's success, the other
girls follow suit, and with this pattern of hysterical, self-serving
accusations, the witch trials get underway.

3. You must understand, sir, that a person is either with this court or he must be counted against it, there be no road between. This is a sharp time, now, a precise time—we live no longer in the dusky afternoon when evil mixed itself with good and befuddled the world. Now, by God's grace, the shining sun is up, and them that fear not light will surely praise it.

This statement, given by Danforth in Act III, aptly sums up the attitude of the authorities toward the witch trials. In his own right, Danforth is an honorable man, but, like everyone else in Salem, he sees the world in black and white. Everything and everyone belongs to either God or the devil. The court and government of Massachusetts, being divinely sanctioned, necessarily belong to God. Thus, anyone who opposes the court's activities cannot be an honest opponent. In a theocracy, one cannot have honest disagreements because God is infallible. Since the court is conducting the witch trials, anyone who questions the trials, such as Proctor or Giles Corey, is the court's enemy. From there, the logic is simple: the court does God's work, and so an enemy of the court *must,* necessarily, be a servant of the devil.

4. A man may think God sleeps, but God sees everything, I
   know it now. I beg you, sir, I beg you—see her what she
   is. . . . She thinks to dance with me on my wife's grave! And
   well she might, for I thought of her softly. God help me,
   I lusted, and there is a promise in such sweat. But it is a
   whore's vengeance. . . .

This quotation is taken from Act III, when Proctor finally breaks
down and confesses his affair with Abigail, after trying, in vain, to
expose her as a fraud without revealing their liaison. Proctor knows
from the beginning that the witch trials constitute nothing more
than a "whore's vengeance"—Abigail's revenge on him for ending
their affair—but he shies away from making that knowledge public
because it would lead to his disgrace. This scene, in the Salem courtroom, marks the climax of the play, in which Proctor's concern for
justice outstrips his concern for his reputation. This re-prioritiza-
tion of values enables him to do what is necessary. But he finds, to
his horror, that his actions come too late: instead of Abigail and the
witch trials being exposed as a sham, Proctor is called a liar and then
accused of witchcraft by the court. His attempt at honesty backfires
and destroys him.

5.   Because it is my name! Because I cannot have another in
     my life! Because I lie and sign myself to lies! Because I am
     not worth the dust on the feet of them that hang! How may
     I live without my name? I have given you my soul; leave me
     my name!

Proctor utters these lines at the end of the play, in Act IV, when he is
wrestling with his conscience over whether to confess to witchcraft
and thereby save himself from the gallows. The judges and Hale
have almost convinced him to do so, but the last stumbling block
is his signature on the confession, which he cannot bring himself to
give. In part, this unwillingness reflects his desire not to dishonor his
fellow prisoners: he would not be able to live with himself knowing
that other innocents died while he quaked at death's door and fled.
More important, it illustrates his obsession with his good name.
Reputation is tremendously important in Salem, where public and
private morality are one and the same. Early in the play, Proctor's
desire to preserve his good name keeps him from testifying against
Abigail. Now, however, he has come to a true understanding of
what a good reputation means and what course of action it neces-
sitates—namely, that he tell the truth, not lie to save himself. "I have
given you my soul; leave me my name!" he rages; this defense of his
name enables him to muster the courage to die, heroically, with his
goodness intact.

QUOTATIONS

KEY FACTS

FULL TITLE
The Crucible

AUTHOR
Arthur Miller

TYPE OF WORK
Play

GENRE
Tragedy, allegory

LANGUAGE
English

TIME AND PLACE WRITTEN
America, early 1950s

DATE OF FIRST PUBLICATION
1953

PUBLISHER
Viking Press

NARRATOR
The play is occasionally interrupted by an omniscient, third-person narrator who fills in the background for the characters.

CLIMAX
John Proctor tells the Salem court that he committed adultery with Abigail Williams.

PROTAGONIST
John Proctor

ANTAGONIST
Abigail Williams

SETTING (TIME)
1692

SETTING (PLACE)
Salem, a small town in colonial Massachusetts

POINT OF VIEW

The Crucible is a play, so the audience and reader are entirely outside the action.

FALLING ACTION

The events from John Proctor's attempt to expose Abigail in Act IV to his decision to die rather than confess at the end of Act IV.

TENSE

Present

FORESHADOWING

The time frame of the play is extremely compressed, and the action proceeds so quickly that there is little time for foreshadowing.

TONE

Serious and tragic—the language is almost biblical.

THEMES

Intolerance; hysteria; reputation

MOTIFS

Empowerment; accusation, confession, legal proceedings in general

SYMBOLS

Though the play itself has very few examples of symbolism beyond typical witchcraft symbols (rats, toads, and bats), the entire play is meant to be symbolic, with its witch trials standing in for the anti-Communist "witch-hunts" of the 1950s.

KEY FACTS

Study Questions

1. *Discuss the role that grudges and personal rivalries play in the witch trial hysteria.*

The trials in *The Crucible* take place against the backdrop of a deeply religious and superstitious society, and most of the characters in the play seem to believe that rooting out witches from their community is God's work. However, there are plenty of simmering feuds and rivalries in the small town that have nothing to do with religion, and many Salem residents take advantage of the trials to express long-held grudges and exact revenge on their enemies. Abigail, the original source of the hysteria, has a grudge against Elizabeth Proctor because Elizabeth fired her after she discovered that Abigail was having an affair with her husband, John Proctor. As the ringleader of the girls whose "visions" prompt the witch craze, Abigail happily uses the situation to accuse Elizabeth and have her sent to jail. Meanwhile, Reverend Parris, a paranoid and insecure figure, begins the play with a precarious hold on his office, and the trials enable him to strengthen his position within the village by making scapegoats of people like Proctor who question his authority.

Among the minor characters, the wealthy, ambitious Thomas Putnam has a bitter grudge against Francis Nurse for a number of reasons: Nurse prevented Putnam's brother-in-law from being elected to the Salem ministry, and Nurse is also engaged in a bitter land dispute with one of Putnam's relatives. In the end, Rebecca, Francis's virtuous wife, is convicted of the supernatural murders of Ann Putnam's dead babies. Thus, the Putnams not only strike a blow against the Nurse family but also gain some measure of twisted satisfaction for the tragedy of seven stillbirths. This bizarre pursuit of "justice" typifies the way that many of the inhabitants approach the witch trials as an opportunity to gain ultimate satisfaction for simmering resentments by convincing themselves that their rivals are beyond wrong, that they are in league with the devil.

2. *How do the witch trials empower individuals who
were previously powerless?*

Salem is a strict, hierarchical, and patriarchal society. The men of
the town have all of the political power and their rule is buttressed
not only by law but also by the supposed sanction of God. In this
society, the lower rungs of the social ladder are occupied by young,
unmarried girls like Abigail, Mary Warren, and Mercy. Powerless in
daily life, these girls find a sudden source of power in their alleged
possession by the devil and hysterical denunciations of their fellow
townsfolk. Previously, the minister and the girls' parents were God's
earthly representatives, but in the fervor of the witch trials, the girls
are suddenly treated as though they have a direct connection to the
divine. A mere accusation from one of Abigail's troop is enough to
incarcerate and convict even important, influential citizens, and the
girls soon become conscious of their newfound power. In Act II,
for instance, Mary Warren defies Proctor's authority, which derives
from his role as her employer, after she becomes an official of the
court, and she even questions his right to give her orders at all.

Even the most despised and downtrodden inhabitant of Salem,
the black slave Tituba suddenly finds herself similarly empowered.
She can voice all of her hostility toward her master, Parris, and it is
simply excused as "suggestions from the devil." At the same time,
she can declare that she has seen "white people" with the devil, thus
(for the first time in her life, probably) giving her power over the
white community. As the fear of falling on the wrong side of God
causes chaos during the brief period of the hysteria and trials, the
social order of Salem is turned on its head.

3.   *How does John Proctor's great dilemma change during
      the course of the play?*

Proctor, the play's tragic hero, has the conscience of an honest man, but he also has a secret flaw—his past affair with Abigail. Her sexual jealousy, accentuated by Proctor's termination of their affair, provides the spark for the witch trials; Proctor thus bears some responsibility for what occurs. He feels that the only way to stop Abigail and the girls from their lies is to confess his adultery. He refrains for a long time from confessing his sin, however, for the sake of his own good name and his wife's honor. Eventually, though, Proctor's attempts to reveal Abigail as a fraud without revealing the crucial information about their affair fail, and he makes a public confession of his sin. But by the time he comes clean, it is too late to stop the craze from running its course, and Proctor himself is arrested and accused of being a witch.

At this point, Proctor faces a new dilemma and wrestles with his conscience over whether to save himself from the gallows with a confession to a sin that he did not commit. The judges and Hale almost convince him to do so, but in the end, he cannot bring himself to sign his confession. Such an action would dishonor his fellow prisoners, who are steadfastly refusing to make false confessions; more important, he realizes that his own soul, his honor, and his honesty are worth more than a cowardly escape from the gallows. He dies and, in doing so, feels that he has finally purged his guilt for his failure to stop the trials when he had the chance. As his wife says, "he have his goodness now."

How to Write Literary Analysis

The Literary Essay: A Step-by-Step Guide

When you read for pleasure, your only goal is enjoyment. You might find yourself reading to get caught up in an exciting story, to learn about an interesting time or place, or just to pass time. Maybe you're looking for inspiration, guidance, or a reflection of your own life. There are as many different, valid ways of reading a book as there are books in the world.

When you read a work of literature in an English class, however, you're being asked to read in a special way: you're being asked to perform *literary analysis*. To analyze something means to break it down into smaller parts and then examine how those parts work, both individually and together. Literary analysis involves examining all the parts of a novel, play, short story, or poem—elements such as character, setting, tone, and imagery—and thinking about how the author uses those elements to create certain effects.

A literary essay isn't a book review: you're not being asked whether or not you liked a book or whether you'd recommend it to another reader. A literary essay also isn't like the kind of book report you wrote when you were younger, where your teacher wanted you to summarize the book's action. A high school- or college-level literary essay asks, "How does this piece of literature actually work?" "How does it do what it does?" and, "Why might the author have made the choices he or she did?"

The Seven Steps

No one is born knowing how to analyze literature; it's a skill you learn and a process you can master. As you gain more practice with this kind of thinking and writing, you'll be able to craft a method that works best for you. But until then, here are seven basic steps to writing a well-constructed literary essay:

> *1. Ask questions*
> *2. Collect evidence*
> *3. Construct a thesis*

4. Develop and organize arguments
5. Write the introduction
6. Write the body paragraphs
7. Write the conclusion

---

1. ASK QUESTIONS

When you're assigned a literary essay in class, your teacher will often provide you with a list of writing prompts. Lucky you! Now all you have to do is choose one. Do yourself a favor and pick a topic that interests you. You'll have a much better (not to mention easier) time if you start off with something you enjoy thinking about. If you are asked to come up with a topic by yourself, though, you might start to feel a little panicked. Maybe you have too many ideas—or none at all. Don't worry. Take a deep breath and start by asking yourself these questions:

- **What struck you?** Did a particular image, line, or scene linger in your mind for a long time? If it fascinated you, chances are you can draw on it to write a fascinating essay.

- **What confused you?** Maybe you were surprised to see a character act in a certain way, or maybe you didn't understand why the book ended the way it did. Confusing moments in a work of literature are like a loose thread in a sweater: if you pull on it, you can unravel the entire thing. Ask yourself why the author chose to write about that character or scene the way he or she did and you might tap into some important insights about the work as a whole.

- **Did you notice any patterns?** Is there a phrase that the main character uses constantly or an image that repeats throughout the book? If you can figure out how that pattern weaves through the work and what the significance of that pattern is, you've almost got your entire essay mapped out.

- **Did you notice any contradictions or ironies?** Great works of literature are complex; great literary essays recognize and explain those complexities. Maybe the title (*Happy Days*) totally disagrees with the book's subject matter (hungry orphans dying in the woods). Maybe the main character acts one way around his family and a completely different way around his friends and associates. If you can find a way to explain a work's contradictory elements, you've got the seeds of a great essay.

At this point, you don't need to know exactly what you're going to say about your topic; you just need a place to begin your exploration. You can help direct your reading and brainstorming by formulating your topic as a *question,* which you'll then try to answer in your essay. The best questions invite critical debates and discussions, not just a rehashing of the summary. Remember, you're looking for something you can *prove or argue* based on evidence you find in the text. Finally, remember to keep the scope of your question in mind: is this a topic you can adequately address within the word or page limit you've been given? Conversely, is this a topic big enough to fill the required length?

Good Questions

"Are Romeo and Juliet's parents responsible for the deaths of their children?"

"Why do pigs keep showing up in Lord of the Flies*?"*

"Are Dr. Frankenstein and his monster alike? How?"

Bad Questions

"What happens to Scout in To Kill a Mockingbird*?"*

"What do the other characters in Julius Caesar *think about Caesar?"*

"How does Hester Prynne in The Scarlet Letter *remind me of my sister?"*

---

2. Collect Evidence

Once you know what question you want to answer, it's time to scour the book for things that will help you answer the question. Don't worry if you don't know what you want to say yet—right now you're just collecting ideas and material and letting it all percolate. Keep track of passages, symbols, images, or scenes that deal with your topic. Eventually, you'll start making connections between these examples and your thesis will emerge.

Here's a brief summary of the various parts that compose each and every work of literature. These are the elements that you will analyze in your essay, and which you will offer as evidence to support your arguments. For more on the parts of literary works, see the Glossary of Literary Terms at the end of this section.

ELEMENTS OF STORY   These are the *what*s of the work—what happens, where it happens, and to whom it happens.

- **Plot:** All of the events and actions of the work.

- **Character:** The people who act and are acted upon in a literary work. The main character of a work is known as the *protagonist.*

- **Conflict:** The central tension in the work. In most cases, the protagonist wants something, while opposing forces (antagonists) hinder the protagonist's progress.

- **Setting:** When and where the work takes place. Elements of setting include location, time period, time of day, weather, social atmosphere, and economic conditions.

- **Narrator:** The person telling the story. The narrator may straightforwardly report what happens, convey the subjective opinions and perceptions of one or more characters, or provide commentary and opinion in his or her own voice.

- **Themes:** The main idea or message of the work—usually an abstract idea about people, society, or life in general. A work may have many themes, which may be in tension with one another.

ELEMENTS OF STYLE   These are the *how*s—how the characters speak, how the story is constructed, and how language is used throughout the work.

- **Structure and organization:** How the parts of the work are assembled. Some novels are narrated in a linear, chronological fashion, while others skip around in time. Some plays follow a traditional three- or five-act structure, while others are a series of loosely connected scenes. Some authors deliberately leave gaps in their works, leaving readers to puzzle out the missing information. A work's structure and organization can tell you a lot about the kind of message it wants to convey.

- **Point of view:** The perspective from which a story is told. In *first-person point of view,* the narrator involves him or herself in the story. ("I went to the store"; "We watched in horror as the bird slammed into the window.") A first-person narrator is usually the protagonist of the work, but not always. In *third-person point of view,* the narrator does not participate in the story. A third-person narrator may closely follow a specific character, recounting that individual character's thoughts or experiences, or it may be what we call an *omniscient* narrator. Omniscient narrators see and know all: they can witness any event in any time or place and are privy to the inner thoughts and feelings of all characters. Remember that the narrator and the author are not the same thing!

- **Diction:** Word choice. Whether a character uses dry, clinical language or flowery prose with lots of exclamation points can tell you a lot about his or her attitude and personality.

- **Syntax:** Word order and sentence construction. Syntax is a crucial part of establishing an author's narrative voice. Ernest Hemingway, for example, is known for writing in very short, straightforward sentences, while James Joyce characteristically wrote in long, incredibly complicated lines.

- **Tone:** The mood or feeling of the text. Diction and syntax often contribute to the tone of a work. A novel written in short, clipped sentences that use small, simple words might feel brusque, cold, or matter-of-fact.

- **Imagery:** Language that appeals to the senses, representing things that can be seen, smelled, heard, tasted, or touched.

- **Figurative language:** Language that is not meant to be interpreted literally. The most common types of figurative language are *metaphors* and *similes,* which compare two unlike things in order to suggest a similarity between them— for example, "All the world's a stage," or "The moon is like a ball of green cheese." (Metaphors say one thing *is* another thing; similes claim that one thing is *like* another thing.)

3. CONSTRUCT A THESIS

When you've examined all the evidence you've collected and know how you want to answer the question, it's time to write your thesis statement. A *thesis* is a claim about a work of literature that needs to be supported by evidence and arguments. The thesis statement is the heart of the literary essay, and the bulk of your paper will be spent trying to prove this claim. A good thesis will be:

- **Arguable.** "*The Great Gatsby* describes New York society in the 1920s" isn't a thesis—it's a fact.

- **Provable through textual evidence.** "*Hamlet* is a confusing but ultimately very well-written play" is a weak thesis because it offers the writer's personal opinion about the book. Yes, it's arguable, but it's not a claim that can be proved or supported with examples taken from the play itself.

- **Surprising.** "Both George and Lenny change a great deal in *Of Mice and Men*" is a weak thesis because it's obvious. A really strong thesis will argue for a reading of the text that is not immediately apparent.

- **Specific.** "Dr. Frankenstein's monster tells us a lot about the human condition" is *almost* a really great thesis statement, but it's still too vague. What does the writer mean by "a lot"? *How* does the monster tell us so much about the human condition?

GOOD THESIS STATEMENTS

Question: In *Romeo and Juliet*, which is more powerful in shaping the lovers' story: fate or foolishness?

Thesis: "Though Shakespeare defines Romeo and Juliet as 'star-crossed lovers' and images of stars and planets appear throughout the play, a closer examination of that celestial imagery reveals that the stars are merely witnesses to the characters' foolish activities and not the causes themselves."

Question: How does the bell jar function as a symbol in Sylvia Plath's *The Bell Jar*?

Thesis: "A bell jar is a bell-shaped glass that has three basic uses: to hold a specimen for observation, to contain gases, and to maintain a vacuum. The bell jar appears in each of these capacities in *The Bell Jar*, Plath's semi-autobiographical novel, and each appearance marks a different stage in Esther's mental breakdown."

Question: Would Piggy in *The Lord of the Flies* make a good island leader if he were given the chance?

Thesis: "Though the intelligent, rational, and innovative Piggy has the mental characteristics of a good leader, he ultimately lacks the social skills necessary to be an effective one. Golding emphasizes this point by giving Piggy a foil in the charismatic Jack, whose magnetic personality allows him to capture and wield power effectively, if not always wisely."

4. DEVELOP AND ORGANIZE ARGUMENTS

The reasons and examples that support your thesis will form the middle paragraphs of your essay. Since you can't really write your thesis statement until you know how you'll structure your argument, you'll probably end up working on steps 3 and 4 at the same time.

There's no single method of argumentation that will work in every context. One essay prompt might ask you to compare and contrast two characters, while another asks you to trace an image through a given work of literature. These questions require different kinds of answers and therefore different kinds of arguments. Below, we'll discuss three common kinds of essay prompts and some strategies for constructing a solid, well-argued case.

TYPES OF LITERARY ESSAYS

- **Compare and contrast**

    Compare and contrast the characters of Huck and Jim in THE ADVENTURES OF HUCKLEBERRY FINN.

    Chances are you've written this kind of essay before. In an academic literary context, you'll organize your arguments the same way you would in any other class. You can either go *subject by subject* or *point by point*. In the former, you'll discuss one character first and then the second. In the latter, you'll choose several traits (attitude toward life, social status, images and metaphors associated with the character) and devote a paragraph to each. You may want to use a mix of these two approaches—for example, you may want to spend a paragraph a piece broadly sketching Huck's and Jim's personalities before transitioning into a paragraph or two that describes a few key points of comparison. This can be a highly effective strategy if you want to make a counterintuitive argument—that, despite seeming to be totally different, the two objects being compared are actually similar in a very important way (or vice versa). Remember that your essay should reveal something fresh or unexpected about the text, so think beyond the obvious parallels and differences.

- **Trace**

    Choose an image—for example, birds, knives, or eyes—and trace that image throughout MACBETH.

    Sounds pretty easy, right? All you need to do is read the play, underline every appearance of a knife in *Macbeth,* and then list them in your essay in the order they appear, right? Well, not exactly. Your teacher doesn't want a simple catalog of examples. He or she wants to see you make *connections* between those examples—that's the difference between summarizing and analyzing. In the *Macbeth* example above, think about the different contexts in which knives appear in the play and to what effect. In *Macbeth,* there are real knives and imagined knives; knives that kill and knives that simply threaten. Categorize and classify your examples to give them some order. Finally, always keep the overall effect in mind. After you choose and analyze your examples, you should come to some greater understanding about the work, as well as your chosen image, symbol, or phrase's role in developing the major themes and stylistic strategies of that work.

- **Debate**

  Is the society depicted in 1984 *good for its citizens?*

  In this kind of essay, you're being asked to debate a moral, ethical, or aesthetic issue regarding the work. You might be asked to judge a character or group of characters (*Is Caesar responsible for his own demise?*) or the work itself (*Is* JANE EYRE *a feminist novel?*). For this kind of essay, there are two important points to keep in mind. First, don't simply base your arguments on your personal feelings and reactions. Every literary essay expects you to read and analyze the work, so search for evidence in the text. What do characters in *1984* have to say about the government of Oceania? What images does Orwell use that might give you a hint about his attitude toward the government? As in any debate, you also need to make sure that you define all the necessary terms before you begin to argue your case. What does it mean to be a "good" society? What makes a novel "feminist"? You should define your terms right up front, in the first paragraph after your introduction.

  Second, remember that strong literary essays make contrary and surprising arguments. Try to think outside the box. In the *1984* example above, it seems like the obvious answer would be no, the totalitarian society depicted in Orwell's novel is *not* good for its citizens. But can you think of any arguments for the opposite side? Even if your final assertion is that the novel depicts a cruel, repressive, and therefore harmful society, acknowledging and responding to the counterargument will strengthen your overall case.

5. Write the Introduction

Your introduction sets up the entire essay. It's where you present your topic and articulate the particular issues and questions you'll be addressing. It's also where you, as the writer, introduce yourself to your readers. A persuasive literary essay immediately establishes its writer as a knowledgeable, authoritative figure.

An introduction can vary in length depending on the overall length of the essay, but in a traditional five-paragraph essay it should be no longer than one paragraph. However long it is, your introduction needs to:

- **Provide any necessary context.** Your introduction should situate the reader and let him or her know what to expect. What book are you discussing? Which characters? What topic will you be addressing?

- **Answer the "So what?" question.** Why is this topic important, and why is your particular position on the topic noteworthy? Ideally, your introduction should pique the reader's interest by suggesting how your argument is surprising or otherwise counterintuitive. Literary essays make unexpected connections and reveal less-than-obvious truths.

- **Present your thesis.** This usually happens at or very near the end of your introduction.

- **Indicate the shape of the essay to come.** Your reader should finish reading your introduction with a good sense of the scope of your essay as well as the path you'll take toward proving your thesis. You don't need to spell out every step, but you do need to suggest the organizational pattern you'll be using.

Your introduction should not:

- **Be vague.** Beware of the two killer words in literary analysis: *interesting* and *important*. Of course the work, question, or example is interesting and important—that's why you're writing about it!

- **Open with any grandiose assertions.** Many student readers think that beginning their essays with a flamboyant statement such as, "Since the dawn of time, writers have been fascinated with the topic of free will," makes them

sound important and commanding. You know what? It
actually sounds pretty amateurish.

- **Wildly praise the work.** Another typical mistake student
  writers make is extolling the work or author. Your teacher
  doesn't need to be told that "Shakespeare is perhaps the
  greatest writer in the English language." You can mention
  a work's reputation in passing—by referring to *The Adventures of Huckleberry Finn* as "Mark Twain's enduring
  classic," for example—but don't make a point of bringing it
  up unless that reputation is key to your argument.

- **Go off-topic.** Keep your introduction streamlined and to
  the point. Don't feel the need to throw in all kinds of bells
  and whistles in order to impress your reader—just get to the
  point as quickly as you can, without skimping on any of the
  required steps.

---

6. WRITE THE BODY PARAGRAPHS

Once you've written your introduction, you'll take the arguments
you developed in step 4 and turn them into your body paragraphs.
The organization of this middle section of your essay will largely be
determined by the argumentative strategy you use, but no matter
how you arrange your thoughts, your body paragraphs need to do
the following:

- **Begin with a strong topic sentence.** Topic sentences are like
  signs on a highway: they tell the reader where they are and
  where they're going. A good topic sentence not only alerts
  readers to what issue will be discussed in the following
  paragraph but also gives them a sense of what argument
  will be made *about* that issue. "Rumor and gossip play an
  important role in *The Crucible*" isn't a strong topic sentence
  because it doesn't tell us very much. "The community's
  constant gossiping creates an environment that allows false
  accusations to flourish" is a much stronger topic sentence—
  it not only tells us *what* the paragraph will discuss (gossip)
  but *how* the paragraph will discuss the topic (by showing
  how gossip creates a set of conditions that leads to the play's
  climactic action).

- **Fully and completely develop a single thought.** Don't skip
  around in your paragraph or try to stuff in too much
  material. Body paragraphs are like bricks: each individual

one needs to be strong and sturdy or the entire structure will collapse. Make sure you have really proven your point before moving on to the next one.

- **Use transitions effectively.** Good literary essay writers know that each paragraph must be clearly and strongly linked to the material around it. Think of each paragraph as a response to the one that precedes it. Use transition words and phrases such as *however, similarly, on the contrary, therefore,* and *furthermore* to indicate what kind of response you're making.

---

7. WRITE THE CONCLUSION

Just as you used the introduction to ground your readers in the topic before providing your thesis, you'll use the conclusion to quickly summarize the specifics learned thus far and then hint at the broader implications of your topic. A good conclusion will:

- **Do more than simply restate the thesis.** If your thesis argued that *The Catcher in the Rye* can be read as a Christian allegory, don't simply end your essay by saying, "And that is why *The Catcher in the Rye* can be read as a Christian allegory." If you've constructed your arguments well, this kind of statement will just be redundant.

- **Synthesize the arguments, not summarize them.** Similarly, don't repeat the details of your body paragraphs in your conclusion. The reader has already read your essay, and chances are it's not so long that they've forgotten all your points by now.

- **Revisit the "So what?" question.** In your introduction, you made a case for why your topic and position are important. You should close your essay with the same sort of gesture. What do your readers know now that they didn't know before? How will that knowledge help them better appreciate or understand the work overall?

- **Move from the specific to the general.** Your essay has most likely treated a very specific element of the work—a single character, a small set of images, or a particular passage. In your conclusion, try to show how this narrow discussion has wider implications for the work overall. If your essay on *To Kill a Mockingbird* focused on the character of Boo Radley, for example, you might want to include a bit in your conclusion about how he fits into the novel's larger message about childhood, innocence, or family life.

- **Stay relevant.** Your conclusion should suggest new directions of thought, but it shouldn't be treated as an opportunity to pad your essay with all the extra, interesting ideas you came up with during your brainstorming sessions but couldn't fit into the essay proper. Don't attempt to stuff in unrelated queries or too many abstract thoughts.

- **Avoid making overblown closing statements.** A conclusion should open up your highly specific, focused discussion, but it should do so without drawing a sweeping lesson about life or human nature. Making such observations may be part of the point of reading, but it's almost always a mistake in essays, where these observations tend to sound overly dramatic or simply silly.

A+ ESSAY CHECKLIST

Congratulations! If you've followed all the steps we've outlined above, you should have a solid literary essay to show for all your efforts. What if you've got your sights set on an A+? To write the kind of superlative essay that will be rewarded with a perfect grade, keep the following rubric in mind. These are the qualities that teachers expect to see in a truly A+ essay. How does yours stack up?

- ✓ Demonstrates a thorough understanding of the book
- ✓ Presents an original, compelling argument
- ✓ Thoughtfully analyzes the text's formal elements
- ✓ Uses appropriate and insightful examples
- ✓ Structures ideas in a logical and progressive order
- ✓ Demonstrates a mastery of sentence construction, transitions, grammar, spelling, and word choice

LITERARY ANALYSIS

Suggested Essay Topics

1. Compare the roles that Elizabeth Proctor and Abigail Williams play in THE CRUCIBLE.

2. Why are Danforth, Hathorne, and the other authorities so resistant to believing the claim that Abigail and the other girls are lying?

3. What kind of government does Salem have? What role does it play in the action?

4. Analyze Reverend Parris. What are his motivations in supporting the witch trials?

5. Discuss the changes that Reverend Hale undergoes in the course of the play.

A+ Student Essay

What role does sex and sexual repression play in
The Crucible?

Part of the enduring appeal of Arthur Miller's *The Crucible* lies in its resonance with various contemporary events. While the play is certainly a critique of the McCarthy era, it can also be read as a commentary on anti-feminism, fascism, or any number of other repressive movements. Miller's play remains so broadly applicable in part because he avoids attributing the Salemites' hysteria to any one specific cause. He does not simply ascribe the witch hunt mania to religious conviction, groupthink, or longstanding feuds. Rather, he suggests that a number of complex causes led to the deaths of innocent people—sexual repression being one such cause.

Abigail's inability to express her sexuality openly is one of the key instigators of the witch hunt. In puritanical 1690s Massachusetts, Abigail's brand of passionate sexuality can find no appropriate outlet. Her nature demands that she be a voracious lover, but her circumstances forbid it. When she falls for John Proctor, she knows that their dalliance cannot possibly have a happy outcome. Proctor will not leave his wife, because divorce would be unthinkable, and he will not continue the affair, because he remains wracked with guilt over what his society considers the grave sin of extramarital sex. Nor can Abigail comfort herself with the knowledge that she will find another lover sooner or later. Desirable men, let alone desirable men willing to sleep with women who are not their wives, are a rarity in Salem. Abigail cannot find relief by talking about her problems, since her behavior, shocking by the standards of the day, would horrify other members of her community. Frustrated at every turn, Abigail turns to violent scheming. When the spells she asks Tituba to perform snowball into a hunt for witches, Abigail sees a chance to get rid of Elizabeth Proctor, the woman she holds responsible for impeding her sexual fulfillment.

The enthusiasm with which Betty and the other girls follow Abigail's lead can also be traced to sexual repression. Society teaches these girls that their physical urges are unnatural, even sinful. Therefore, the girls vent their feelings in secret, with each other. While we never learn precisely what happens in the woods, Miller implies that the girls' meetings have an erotic component. In his notes in

Act One, Miller likens the meetings to the "*klatches* in Europe, where the daughters of the towns would assemble at night and . . . give themselves to love." While there is nothing sinister about what Abigail and the girls do in the woods, there is something sinister about the girls' reaction to their own behavior. They believe they are doing something horribly wrong, and when they are threatened with exposure, they grow hysterical. So convinced are they of the inherent wickedness of sexuality that they would rather send people to their deaths than confess to their own sexual behavior.

Elizabeth Proctor's shame over her husband's sexuality and her incapacity to discuss it openly help doom Proctor to death. Beyond her horror at her husband's sinful adulterous behavior, Elizabeth feels an aversion to exposing that behavior in court. In part, her reluctance stems from a charitable desire to protect Proctor's reputation. In addition, though, Elizabeth is deeply ashamed of what her husband has done. She is a notably truthful woman, whom lying causes almost physical pain. Yet she would rather lie under oath than admit she is married to an adulterer. By inadvertently casting her husband as a liar, Elizabeth helps the cause of those eager to damn him as a witch.

Miller suggests that the consequences of sexual repression can be as dire as the consequences of religious intolerance or fear of outsiders. In addition to its impassioned plea for individual rights and measured political discourse, *The Crucible* makes a strong case for the open acknowledgement and analysis of sexual desires.

GLOSSARY OF LITERARY TERMS

ANTAGONIST

The entity that acts to frustrate the goals of the *protagonist*. The antagonist is usually another *character* but may also be a non-human force.

ANTIHERO / ANTIHEROINE

A *protagonist* who is not admirable or who challenges notions of what should be considered admirable.

CHARACTER

A person, animal, or any other thing with a personality that appears in a *narrative*.

CLIMAX

The moment of greatest intensity in a text or the major turning point in the *plot*.

CONFLICT

The central struggle that moves the *plot* forward. The conflict can be the *protagonist*'s struggle against fate, nature, society, or another person.

FIRST-PERSON POINT OF VIEW

A literary style in which the *narrator* tells the story from his or her own *point of view* and refers to himself or herself as "I." The narrator may be an active participant in the story or just an observer.

HERO / HEROINE

The principal *character* in a literary work or *narrative*.

IMAGERY

Language that brings to mind sense-impressions, representing things that can be seen, smelled, heard, tasted, or touched.

MOTIF

A recurring idea, structure, contrast, or device that develops or informs the major *themes* of a work of literature.

NARRATIVE

A story.

NARRATOR

The person (sometimes a *character*) who tells a story; the *voice* assumed by the writer. The narrator and the author of the work of literature are not the same person.

PLOT

The arrangement of the events in a story, including the sequence in which they are told, the relative emphasis they are given, and the causal connections between events.

POINT OF VIEW

The *perspective* that a *narrative* takes toward the events it describes.

PROTAGONIST

The main *character* around whom the story revolves.

SETTING

The location of a *narrative* in time and space. Setting creates mood or atmosphere.

SUBPLOT

A secondary *plot* that is of less importance to the overall story but may serve as a point of contrast or comparison to the main plot.

SYMBOL

An object, *character,* figure, or color that is used to represent an abstract idea or concept. Unlike an *emblem,* a symbol may have different meanings in different contexts.

SYNTAX

The way the words in a piece of writing are put together to form lines, phrases, or clauses; the basic structure of a piece of writing.

THEME

A fundamental and universal idea explored in a literary work.

TONE

The author's attitude toward the subject or *characters* of a story or poem or toward the reader.

VOICE

An author's individual way of using language to reflect his or her own personality and attitudes. An author communicates voice through *tone, diction,* and *syntax.*

A Note on Plagiarism

Plagiarism—presenting someone else's work as your own—rears its ugly head in many forms. Many students know that copying text without citing it is unacceptable. But some don't realize that even if you're not quoting directly, but instead are paraphrasing or summarizing, *it is plagiarism* unless you cite the source.

Here are the most common forms of plagiarism:

- Using an author's phrases, sentences, or paragraphs without citing the source
- Paraphrasing an author's ideas without citing the source
- Passing off another student's work as your own

How do you steer clear of plagiarism? You should *always* acknowledge all words and ideas that aren't your own by using quotation marks around verbatim text or citations like footnotes and endnotes to note another writer's ideas. For more information on how to give credit when credit is due, ask your teacher for guidance or visit www.sparknotes.com.

Review & Resources

Quiz

1. What kind of government does Salem have in *The Crucible?*

   A. Democracy
   B. Theocracy
   C. Monarchy
   D. Kleptocracy

2. What is Parris's position in Salem?

   A. Governor
   B. Judge
   C. Minister
   D. Bailiff

3. Before the play begins, what did Parris catch his daughter and other girls doing?

   A. Trying to run away from home
   B. Dancing in the forest
   C. Reading Catholic tracts
   D. Conducting a black mass in the church

4. Why did Elizabeth Proctor fire Abigail?

   A. Abigail was too proud.
   B. Abigail didn't work hard enough.
   C. Abigail dressed like a prostitute.
   D. Abigail was having an affair with John Proctor.

5. As the play opens, whom has Parris asked to come to Salem?

   A. Judge Danforth
   B. Reverend Hale
   C. Tituba
   D. John Proctor

6.   What is John Proctor's chief complaint against Parris's sermons?

    A.   They focus too much on fire and brimstone.
    B.   They are too long.
    C.   They are heretical.
    D.   They are too short.

7.   What does Mrs. Putnam blame on witchcraft?

    A.   Her husband's cancer
    B.   The death of seven of her children in infancy
    C.   Bad weather
    D.   Raids by natives

8.   Who is the first person that Abigail claims practiced witchcraft?

    A.   Tituba
    B.   John Proctor
    C.   Reverend Hale
    D.   Mary Warren

9.   In Act II, what does Mary Warren give to Elizabeth Proctor when she returns home from the trials?

    A.   A cake
    B.   A bonnet
    C.   A kiss
    D.   A little doll

10.   What news does Mary Warren bring from Salem?

    A.   That someone accused Elizabeth of witchcraft
    B.   That the witch trials have ended
    C.   That someone accused John Proctor of witchcraft
    D.   That Reverend Hale is ill

11. Which commandment does John Proctor forget when Reverend Hale quizzes him?

    A. Thou shalt not kill.
    B. Thou shalt not commit adultery.
    C. Honor thy mother and father.
    D. Thou shalt not covet.

12. Whom do Ezekiel Cheever and Herrick, the marshal, come to the Proctor home to arrest?

    A. John Proctor
    B. Reverend Hale
    C. Mary Warren
    D. Elizabeth Proctor

13. To what does John Proctor convince Mary Warren to testify?

    A. That the girls are only pretending to be possessed
    B. That Abigail is a witch
    C. That Hale is a warlock
    D. That he and Abigail slept together

14. Who is in charge of the court?

    A. Giles Corey
    B. Danforth
    C. Hale
    D. Parris

15. Why will Elizabeth not be hanged if she is found guilty?

    A. Because she is a woman
    B. Because the Puritans do not allow capital punishment
    C. Because she is pregnant
    D. Because John Proctor is well respected

16. On what charge is Giles Corey arrested?

    A. Witchcraft
    B. Murder
    C. Contempt of court
    D. Slander

REVIEW & RESOURCES

17. When Mary Warren testifies against them, what do Abigail and her troop of girls do?

    A.   They all confess.
    B.   They attack her.
    C.   They claim that Mary is bewitching them.
    D.   They claim that John Proctor has bewitched Mary.

18. What does John Proctor do, in a desperate attempt to foil Abigail?

    A.   He tells the court about his affair with her.
    B.   He accuses her of witchcraft.
    C.   He tries to kill her.
    D.   He tells the court that Abigail is a man dressed as a woman.

19. Who is brought in to corroborate John Proctor's claims about Abigail?

    A.   Elizabeth Proctor
    B.   Rebecca Nurse
    C.   Mary Warren
    D.   Parris

20. What does Elizabeth do when called upon to testify?

    A.   Keeps silent
    B.   Tells a lie
    C.   Tells the truth
    D.   Kills herself

21. What does the court do with John Proctor?

    A.   It frees him and sends him home.
    B.   It orders him stoned to death.
    C.   It exiles him to Maine.
    D.   It arrests and tries him for witchcraft.

REVIEW & RESOURCES

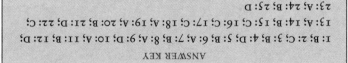

22. When John Proctor is facing death, what does Hale urge him to do?

    A. Kill himself
    B. Blame someone else
    C. Confess, even though he is innocent
    D. Refuse to confess

23. Why does Proctor retract his confession?

    A. Because the officials demand that he sign his name to it
    B. Because Hale asks him to
    C. Because new evidence has come to light
    D. Because Abigail confesses

24. What does Abigail do at the end of the play?

    A. She kills herself.
    B. She flees Salem, after robbing her uncle.
    C. She is hanged.
    D. She is revealed as a witch.

25. What ultimately happens to John Proctor?

    A. He is freed.
    B. He kills himself.
    C. He escapes from prison and flees to Virginia.
    D. He is hanged.

SUGGESTIONS FOR FURTHER READING

BOYER, PAUL, and STEPHEN NISSBAUM. *Salem Possessed: The Social Origins of Witchcraft.* Cambridge, MA: Harvard University Press, 1974.

CARSON, NEIL. *Arthur Miller.* New York: Grove Press, 1982.

FERRES, JOHN, ed. *Twentieth Century Interpretations of* THE CRUCIBLE. Englewood Cliffs, NJ: Prentice-Hall, 1972.

HAYES, RICHARD. "Hysteria and Ideology in *The Crucible.*" *Commonwealth* 57 (February 1953), p. 498.

MARTINE, JAMES J. THE CRUCIBLE: *Politics, Property, and Pretense.* New York: Twayne Publishers, 1993.

MARTIN, ROBERT A., ed. *Arthur Miller: New Perspectives.* Englewood Cliffs, NJ: Prentice-Hall, 1982.

MILLER, ARTHUR. *The Crucible.* New York: Penguin Books, 1995.

REVIEW & RESOURCES

SparkNotes Literature Guides

1984
The Adventures of Huckleberry Finn
The Adventures of Tom Sawyer
The Aeneid
All Quiet on the Western Front
And Then There Were None
Angela's Ashes
Animal Farm
Anna Karenina
Anne of Green Gables
Anthem
As I Lay Dying
The Awakening
The Bean Trees
Beloved
Beowulf
Billy Budd
Black Boy
Bless Me, Ultima
The Bluest Eye
Brave New World
The Brothers Karamazov
The Call of the Wild
Candide
The Canterbury Tales
Catch-22
The Catcher in the Rye
The Chocolate War
The Chosen
Cold Sassy Tree
The Color Purple
The Count of Monte Cristo
Crime and Punishment
The Crucible
Cry, the Beloved Country
Cyrano de Bergerac
David Copperfield
Death of a Salesman
Death of Socrates
Diary of a Young Girl

A Doll's House
Don Quixote
Dr. Faustus
Dr. Jekyll and Mr. Hyde
Dracula
Edith Hamilton's Mythology
Emma
Ethan Frome
Fahrenheit 451
A Farewell to Arms
The Fellowship of the Rings
Flowers for Algernon
For Whom the Bell Tolls
The Fountainhead
Frankenstein
The Giver
The Glass Menagerie
The Good Earth
The Grapes of Wrath
Great Expectations
The Great Gatsby
Grendel
Gulliver's Travels
Hamlet
The Handmaid's Tale
Hard Times
Heart of Darkness
Henry IV, Part I
Henry V
Hiroshima
The Hobbit
The House on Mango Street
I Know Why the Caged Bird Sings
The Iliad
The Importance of Being Earnest
Inferno
Invisible Man
Jane Eyre
Johnny Tremain
The Joy Luck Club
Julius Caesar

The Jungle
The Killer Angels
King Lear
The Last of the Mohicans
Les Misérables
A Lesson Before Dying
Little Women
Lord of the Flies
Macbeth
Madame Bovary
The Merchant of Venice
A Midsummer Night's Dream
Moby-Dick
Much Ado About Nothing
My Ántonia
Narrative of the Life of Frederick Douglass
Native Son
The New Testament
Night
The Odyssey
Oedipus Plays
Of Mice and Men
The Old Man and the Sea
The Old Testament
Oliver Twist
The Once and Future King
One Flew Over the Cuckoo's Nest
One Hundred Years of Solitude
Othello
Our Town
The Outsiders
Paradise Lost
The Pearl
The Picture of Dorian Gray
Poe's Short Stories
A Portrait of the Artist as a Young Man

Pride and Prejudice
The Prince
A Raisin in the Sun
The Red Badge of Courage
The Republic
The Return of the King
Richard III
Robinson Crusoe
Romeo and Juliet
Scarlet Letter
A Separate Peace
Silas Marner
Sir Gawain and the Green Knight
Slaughterhouse-Five
Song of Solomon
The Sound and the Fury
The Stranger
A Streetcar Named Desire
The Sun Also Rises
A Tale of Two Cities
The Taming of the Shrew
The Tempest
Tess of the d'Urbervilles
The Things They Carried
The Two Towers
Their Eyes Were Watching God
Things Fall Apart
To Kill a Mockingbird
Treasure Island
Twelfth Night
Ulysses
Uncle Tom's Cabin
Walden
War and Peace
Wuthering Heights
A Yellow Raft in Blue Water

Visit sparknotes.com for many more!